Bridges Out
of the Past

A Survivor's Lessons
on Resilience

Ria Story

WHAT PEOPLE ARE SAYING ABOUT RIA AND HER STORY

"I want to start by saying thank you...You made me want to try at life because you made me realize that you can make it anywhere you want, no matter where or what you are from. THANK YOU SO MUCH!" JONATHAN, HIGH SCHOOL STUDENT

"Ria's book (Beyond Bound and Broken) is full of hope and inspiration, and she shows us that despite experiencing horrific trauma as a young adult, that if we choose to, we can get past anything with the attitude that we bring to our life...Her book is full of wonderful quotes and wisdom." MADELEINE BLACK, AUTHOR OF UNBROKEN

"I am using your material to empower myself and my female clients. Thanks for sharing your story and a wonderful journey of growth." SUE QUIGLEY, LICENSED CLINICAL THERAPIST

"Very few 'victims' would be willing to share such a personal story. However, nothing about Ria is average. She chose to rise above her painful past and now positions it in a way to offer hope and healing to others who've been through unspeakable abuse. Ria's Faith and marriage keep her grounded as she reveals the solid foundation which helps her stand as an overcomer. Read this story and find yourself and your own story strengthened." KARY OBERBRUNNER, AUTHOR AND FOUNDER OF AUTHOR ACADEMY ELITE, ON *RIA'S STORY FROM ASHES TO BEAUTY*

"Thank you, Ria, for bringing our conference to a close. You were definitely an inspiration to all of us! Awesome Job!" MELINDA, PRESIDENT AGS

"I was truly inspired by your presentation and the life lessons taught." JENNIFER, CONFERENCE ATTENDEE

"Beyond Bound and Broken is a deeply inspirational book; one that will stay with you for years to come. The lessons are deep, yet practical, and her advice leads to clear solutions. This is a profoundly hopeful book. We all face pain, difficulty, and doubt but with resilience, we can lead vital, flourishing lives. Ria's story although sometimes painfully difficult to read because of the trials she endured is a story of great courage and compassion both for herself as victim and for those who betrayed her. Forgiveness is a strong theme as is courage. I would highly recommend this book to anyone who is struggling to move forward after experiencing a great trial." AMAZON CUSTOMER

"...it was awesome! Ria has a real gift. I came away with so many helpful tools! Thank you, Ria." STEFANIE, CONFERENCE ATTENDEE

"May God continue to bless your efforts. Your triumph is a great joy, and a gift to all that would hear or read it."
LOUIS O., HUMAN RIGHTS ADVOCATE

"What an inspiration you are to all of us especially the women audience. Your book is a clear example & step by step guide on how to become an effective leader. It is so easy to read and simple yet meaningful which is the beauty of this book."
K. POONWALA, CUSTOMER SUCCESS MANAGER, ON *LEADERSHIP GEMS FOR WOMEN*

"What a great read! Thank you for such an inspiring and heartfelt book. Keep up the excellent work!"
A. RAMIREZ ON *LEADERSHIP GEMS FOR WOMEN*

"I wanted to thank you for your book Leadership Gems (for Women). Your insights are right on target and this will help me in my work!" S. GUERARD, ON *LEADERSHIP GEMS FOR WOMEN*

"I truly enjoyed the encouraging words you had to share. I admire you so much, and you are such a dynamic and motivational speaker. You are a true inspiration."
LAURA, CONFERENCE ATTENDEE

"Your story is so inspiring, and I find it so amazing to see what you have done with your life! You are truly an inspiration to me, and for other young women like me who have also overcome struggles...You are living proof that no matter where you come from, or what has happened in your past, it does NOT define you, and it does not define your future."
EMMA, PUBLIC RELATIONS SPECIALIST

"Ria's openness to speak of her unique story is commendable...I recommend reading this inspiring story to anyone who wants reassurance that they can, and will, overcome whatever obstacles life throws their way." MATT WATSON, REGIONAL SALES MANAGER, ON *RIA'S STORY FROM ASHES TO BEAUTY*

"I have actually read this book twice. I took many things in the book and have applied them to my own life. I greatly admire Ria for her strength and in reading this book I found some strength within myself. Thank you, Ria, for sharing your story." ANNA B., AMAZON CUSTOMER, ON *RIA'S STORY FROM ASHES TO BEAUTY*

"Ria's vulnerability and larger than life attitude is magnetic. She is not just a survivor but a woman that thrives, as evidenced by her courage to live out her dreams in spite of what she endured. Her resolve and dependence on God is to be emulated!"
DEBI MARKLAND, VP WELLS FARGO BANK, ON *RIA'S STORY FROM ASHES TO BEAUTY*

"Thank you for helping make our event a success!"
DAVID, DIRECTOR OF SERVICES EGOV/BOARDDOCS

CONTENTS

DEDICATION

This book is dedicated to those who are ready to discover
the difference between *"I didn't die,"*
and *"I learned to live again."*

We all have a story to tell. What happens to us in life is
not as important as what we do and who we
become from that moment on.

What matters is the rest of your story.

INTRODUCTION
BRIDGES OUT OF THE PAST AND INTO THE FUTURE

"I am not a product of my circumstances. I am a product of my decisions."

~ Stephen R. Covey

There once was a 12 year old little girl who carried a dark secret inside. Shy, quiet, and lonely, she didn't have many friends, and she was afraid to talk to the ones she had. She was afraid someone might find out what daddy was doing when he tucked her in at night. He told her not to tell anyone because they wouldn't understand.

She didn't understand.

I still don't understand.

It progressed as I got older. By the time I was 17, my father was regularly having sex with me and would bargain with me for sexual favors in return for something like an outing with my friends. He started sharing me with other men, so in his words, he could *"help me find an ultimate experience in life."* An *"ultimate experience"* apparently meant lots of things to him.

One time, it meant taking nude pictures of me riding my horse. One time, it meant tying me up naked, putting a gag in my mouth, and beating me with a riding crop until I was black and blue. One time, it meant watching another man have sex with me. And then, they changed places.

Life was almost not worth living. I considered a razor blade and a tub of warm water to end it.

I left home at 19. I left behind the father who sexually abused me for seven years. And, I left behind the mother who blamed me for it. I left with a few pillowcases and one duffle bag stuffed with some clothes, and not much else. I left without a job or a car. Because I was homeschooled, I didn't even have a high school diploma. I had never been to a real school.

After leaving home, I built a wall around what had happened to me. To survive, I locked my past up tight behind the wall and threw away the key.

Mark Twain said, *"The two greatest days in your life are the day you are born and the day you discover why."* On August 14, 2013, I found my *"why"* and shared my story publicly for the first time. In doing so, I shattered the bonds of shame, fear, and false guilt that had held me captive for 20 long years, since I was 12 years old. I broke down the wall I had built, finally realizing it was holding me prisoner to the past.

In life, we all experience pain, grief, and loss. Resilience is learning not only to survive, but also to thrive. Resilience is rising from the ashes of what happened to us and becoming more brilliant because of the flames. Resilience is the difference between *"I didn't die,"* and *"I learned to live again."*

Resilience is learning to build a bridge out of the past, instead of a building a wall around it. There isn't a *"hierarchy"* on human suffering. If you have gone through, or are going through, something painful, difficult, sad, or tough, it hurts. I don't share my story, so you will think *"Gee, I don't have it as bad as she did, so I don't have the right to complain."* I share my story, so you will know I have overcome what I went through and to let you know you can overcome what you've been through.

I share much of my personal story in my books, *Ria's Story From Ashes To Beauty* and *Beyond Bound and Broken: A Journey of Healing and Resilience*. I revealed my story in different ways for different reasons in those two books. I also have other books that contain parts of my story to support the lessons I share in those. If you have already read any of those books, you will know some of my story already. However, this book is by far my most vulnerable work. That's not an accident. I know it's an intense read. Believe me, it's much more intense to write it than it is to read it. Only when I'm sharing my struggles can I use my story to motivate you, inspire you, and give you hope.

I know my ability to reach you, inspire you, and help you is limited if I'm not willing to be vulnerable, authentic, and transparent. Therefore, I'm about to share some of my most painful memories as well as some of my greatest joys. Ironically, when we share joy, we multiply it. And when we share pain, we minimize it.

In the first section of this book, I will share several chapters of my personal story in chronological order to provide you with perspective, a bit of insight, and the foundation to support the following sections.

In the second section, I will use the acronym RISE to reveal my four-step process that will help you intentionally become more resilient.

In the third section, I will use small chapters filled with stories and lessons on resilience supported by my thoughts on overcoming specific issues such as fear, shame, pain, bitterness, and hate. Carl Rogers said, *"What is most personal is most universal."* These are all topics I've dealt with personally. They are also the topics others ask me about most often.

Since the day I first shared my story publicly, thousands of people from around the world have shared with me how my story has inspired them. What inspires them most isn't the story of my past – it's how I have chosen to respond to what happened to me.

John C. Maxwell said, *"There are people who've had it better than you and done worse. And, there are people who've had it worse than you and done better. The circumstances really have nothing to do with getting over your personal history. Past hurts can make you bitter or better—the choice is yours."*

Everyone has a story of adversity. We can all relate to the struggle of staying positive, hopeful, and inspired in the face of adversity. The struggle is real. It's a struggle because the choice to let go, move on, and build our bridge out of the past is a choice we often struggle to make. As psychologist and Holocaust survivor Dr. Edith Eger said in her book, *The Choice*, *"Time doesn't heal. It's what you do with the time. Healing is possible when we choose to take responsibility, when we choose to take risks, and finally, when we choose to release the wound, to let go of the past or the grief."*

If there weren't other options, there wouldn't be a struggle because we wouldn't have any other choice. For example, you won't have to struggle with the decision to process the oxygen you breathe today – you don't have a choice. It will happen. However, you may or may not struggle to choose a positive outlook today because there are other options. And sometimes, those other options are easier. Often, the more difficult choice is the better one.

Resilience requires us to look at adversity as an opportunity to become stronger. Resilience is realizing our circumstances don't define us because we always have the freedom to choose our mindset, attitude, and outlook.

With the knowledge that we can make choices comes the responsibility of choosing well. Certainly at times, it's easy to pretend we don't have a choice while making excuses for why we can't overcome something.

But, excuses won't take you to where you want to be in life. We can take what life hands us and be bitter about it or become better because of it.

Your life story isn't about what happened to you. It's about what you did and who you became from that moment on. What matters is the rest of your story, and you will add a paragraph to it one choice at a time.

PART I:
RIA'S STORY

CHAPTER ONE
IN THE BEGINNING

"Hardship often prepares an ordinary person for an extraordinary destiny."

~ C. S. Lewis

In the beginning, it seemed innocent enough. Growing up, I was *"Daddy's little princess."* And like many little girls, I thought my daddy was the best dad in the world.

I was seven years old when my parents bought land in the country. They spent the summer driving there almost daily as we worked to clear the land where they planned to build our home. They built it themselves. When we finally moved in, the house was unfinished. But, my brother and I weren't old enough to care.

The interior walls were only bare studs. Camping out in our sleeping bags seemed like an adventure at first. We had a raw plywood counter in the kitchen that the sink and stove sat on. There was one wood burning stove in the corner of the living room to provide the heat for the house, and it never seemed to warm the second story where the only shower was located. There was a big attic fan but no air conditioning.

For years, until we got a few air conditioning units for the windows, I burned up in the summer. I would find myself sweating at night even though I was on top of the sheets. And, I froze in the winter until I got a space heater for my room. I remember trying to get my numb fingers warm by the stove. The house wasn't sealed up well either. One summer when thousands of millipedes swarmed the house, hundreds of them found a way to crawl inside. We were stepping on them barefoot, picking them out of our shoes, and brushing them off of the furniture.

My parents did most of the work to finish the house themselves, but we all pitched in and tried to help. We made a lot of progress, but it was still unfinished when I left home 12 years later at age 19.

I began attending a private Christian kindergarten when I was four, but my parents decided there was too much satanic influence in private and public education. Or, too much governmental control, which in their eyes amounted to about the same thing. So, my brother and I were homeschooled through all 12 grades. There were a few families in our small social circle that also homeschooled their children, but our peers were few and geographically far between. In the 1980's, homeschooling was a bit unusual. We also lacked the social support systems available to many homeschooled youth today.

Although I was raised in a *"Christian"* home, my parents stopped attending church regularly when I was six or seven. My father would hold home church services, sometimes with other families, but mostly only with our family. He would lecture us for hours on the Bible and provide his interpretation of what it meant to him. His version of Christian living was a set of impossible rules to live by, to fall short of, and that required us to ask for forgiveness whenever we broke them, but he was proud of how righteous he thought he was.

He didn't believe in paying taxes, having insurance, or having social security numbers. He bought quite a few guns and stocked ammunition to prepare for the day the government came to *"get us."*

My father looked down on anyone and everyone who didn't live by his version of Christianity and had no tolerance for the opinions and perspectives of others. One time, he allowed some Mormon believers to come visit and share what they believed with us. He was nice enough while they were there. But once they left, he spent hours ridiculing them and searching for scripture to discount everything they had said.

My father was the dictator in our world. He liked to call himself a king and at times demanded obedience to extremely strict rules. One of his rules was that my mother always had to be home by 5 p.m. Since she was chronically late, somewhat absentminded, and always disorganized, this rule often caused us to cut short visits with friends or family. She would then speed home to try to make it home in time, all while hysterically screaming about how he was going to be so mad at her. And, he was mad when she was even one minute late.

Our home life was a roller coaster. Up when things were going well for my father and down when they weren't. Little things would send him into a raging fit, and my mother was frequently the object of his frustrations. Though very creative, she wasn't good at organizing or managing anything.

She often became hysterical over her inability to complete simple housekeeping tasks. Mounds of dirty laundry would pile up. We would completely run out of clean clothes before she got around to washing. I took on many of the household chores at a young age. My father even paid me a small allowance for it.

He encouraged me and my brother to look down on mom. In fact, more than once, the three of us had a *"family"* meeting to decide if she would be allowed to remain a part of our family. She couldn't have been happy. She threatened to leave on a regular basis and packed her bags more than once. However, she always remained. By the time I was a teenager, she was sleeping in the living room on the sofa. When the four of us traveled in the car as a family, my father expected me to ride up front while my mother rode in the back with my brother.

Mom didn't work and dad was self-employed, working as a contractor to build houses and custom cabinets. We also had a home business selling educational books and products. Occasionally, mom would travel to conferences to sell products to other homeschoolers. Most of the time, my brother would go with her. I always wanted to go, but dad usually wanted me to stay home.

I was about 12 when my father began having conversations with me about sex. Mom was never around or involved in any of these conversations. At first, I didn't think it was unusual because dad always handled the *"important"* conversations in our family. This didn't seem any different at first.

My father very clearly explained what sex was, how it worked, and how God had created women for men. He also started telling me how divorce and infidelity in marriage were wrong. He continued further down that path and began telling me *"his needs"* weren't being met because my mother wasn't meeting them.

Mom would be sent to run errands or something, and my father would often tell her to take my brother with her. He intentionally created those opportunities to be alone with me and talk about sex. At first, all of our talks were about how I needed to be pure and stay away from boys until he was able to find the *"Right man sent by God."*

Later, the talks started to focus on how a woman was designed by God to specifically meet a man's needs. My father told me that was why I was created too. I remember feeling ashamed talking about things like that. But, I didn't know what to do.

Then, he started telling me a father-daughter relationship was supposed to be close in every way, emotionally as well as physically. I remember my father saying I was supposed to give my heart to him *"for safekeeping,"* but I was confused as to why that also meant in a physical way.

One day while my mom and brother were away, my father and I were sitting in the living room having one of our *"talks."* He started telling me how wonderful it was that I was the perfect daughter and so close to him. He took me upstairs, and he kept telling me how God intended for daughters to belong to daddies. He said if I would trust him, he would make sure I lived up to what God wanted. He explained how I was supposed to fill in since my mother wasn't being a proper wife anymore. He told me I would also be fulfilling God's purpose for my life by helping him avoid committing adultery. He said it wouldn't be a sin if I helped him. He then began to take off my clothes while telling me I was the perfect daughter.

After that day, my father began regularly having very frank conversations with me about sex. Sometimes, he would take me with him in the car to talk about sex and *"his needs."* Every time we were alone, he would talk about sex, *"his needs,"* and me. He would tell me how sexy I was, how beautiful I was, and how lucky some man would be to have me.

He always talked about other women too, even my friends who were also my age. He would make remarks about their physical attributes to me. He even commented about a little girl we saw dressed up like a cowgirl at a horse show. She was probably only four or five, but she was dressed very cute in a hat and skirt. He mentioned how her mother *"Knew what she was doing."*

I was taught women should be sexy and sexual to please men. He always wanted me to look good for him and made me wear my clothes too tight to show off my body.

Next, the touching started. At first, it was just him touching me. He would lay me down on their bed and rub lotion on me, gradually getting closer to the areas I knew no one else should be touching. As always, I didn't know how to stop him.

It wasn't long before he wanted me to start touching him as well. First, while he was wearing his shorts. Then later, he began taking them off.

He always made a big deal about taking me one step further. He would tell me how our relationship was so special, and no one else would understand how close we were. He made sure I knew not to tell anyone.

As the months passed, he taught me how to please him sexually with my hands. However, that alone wasn't enough. He also made me tell him sexual fantasy stories and made me help him masturbate while having me lie naked beside him.

He continuously pressured me to become very graphic and more detailed with the stories he made me tell. Then, he made me start including my friends in the stories. When I was allowed to have a friend spend the night, he expected me to *"tell him a story"* that included her the following night after she had gone home. He wanted the story to include what she was wearing, what we were doing together, and what he was doing to us.

I was expected to do these things to him and for him regularly – nearly every night. He always told my mother he was *"tucking me in"* and always locked the door, just in case, but I don't think she ever tried to come in.

When mom was gone from the house, my father would show me pornographic movies, pictures, and magazines while he was *"teaching me to be a better wife."* He especially liked bondage type pornography. He rented the movie *9 ½ Weeks* and watched it with me. Then, like in the movie, he bought a riding crop to spank me.

He ordered lingerie for me from catalogs – looking through them with me and picking out what he wanted. Frederick's of Hollywood was his favorite. He had Playboy magazines regularly and would read them to me while looking at the pictures of the women and talking to me about them. He told me if I ever decided to appear nude in a magazine, he hoped it would be Playboy. He also told me I wasn't going to be allowed to date any boys because *"my heart belonged to him."*

I started having nightmares.

CHAPTER TWO
BOUND AND BROKEN

"We are products of our past, but we don't have to be prisoners of it."

~ Rick Warren

If you look at pictures of me when I was growing up, especially those where I was with friends, I was often dressed in the revealing clothes my father had bought for me. One year, he bought me a sheer blouse with a glittery bra and made me wear it to our family's Christmas dinner.

He taunted his relationship with me, almost as if he was daring anyone to say something. No one ever did which only emboldened him. I can remember being made to sit on his lap around others or at family dinners when I was 15, 16, and even older. He would hold hands with me in public everywhere we went. He always made a big deal of me being his *"princess."* He wanted everyone to know I belonged to him.

My father started bargaining with me whenever I wanted something or wanted to do something.

If I needed horse feed, I would ask for money to buy it. He would refuse to give me the money until I did something to please him sexually. If I wanted to do something with a friend, I had to do something sexual for him in order to earn the privilege. He said if I wanted something, I had to ask. He told me the only way to ask was to *"make 'my man' feel good first."* Then, and only then, could I ask. I had to please him first.

He always said he was training me to be a wife, but I realize now he was training me to be the wife he wished he had. But, I wasn't his wife. I would never be his wife, and I didn't want to be his wife. Nor did I want to be the sex slave he was grooming me to be.

In 1996, some friends joined a local water ski team,

and I was invited to participate. I was 15 and desperate for social contact with others outside our family.

My father said there would be too many opportunities for people to be a bad influence on me. I begged and pleaded. Finally, he told me if I would make him feel good enough he would let me go. He had been pressuring me for months to perform oral sex on him. He realized he finally had something I wanted bad enough and immediately used it against me until I overcame my reluctance to please him as he wanted.

However, he had simply used, abused, and manipulated me once again for his own personal pleasure. Ultimately, he refused to let me join the team. *"Too many guys around,"* he said.

He bought a Polaroid camera when I was 15, and started taking nude pictures of me. One time, he took me outside while mom and my brother were away and made me ride my horse naked, so he could take pictures. He always made me swim naked in our pool when we were alone. Since we lived so far off the main road, he could easily hear if someone was driving our way well before they got to us.

My father was always taking pictures of me and made me pose in the ways that pleased him. He even kept a picture on his desk of me wearing high heels and a bikini. He didn't care if anyone saw it either. I think I was 16 in the picture. No one who saw it said anything.

He kept a photo album of all the nude pictures he had taken of me in my bedroom. He thought that was the best place to keep it hidden from my mom. Later on, when he started contacting other men on the internet, he would often scan and send them the nude pictures of me.

My father said he regretted not starting our relationship earlier, so he could have watched me develop pubic hair, breasts, and *"grow from a girl into a woman."*

As the months and years passed, he wanted, demanded, and expected more and more from me. I was pressured to always reassure him I wanted what he was doing to me. If I showed the slightest hesitation, he said he was having a *"breakdown."* He said he would be damned to hell if I didn't want his attention. He told me as long as I wanted it, it wasn't wrong. In this way, he emotionally blackmailed me, so I would reassure him. He repeatedly said no one else would understand our special relationship, so I shouldn't tell anyone.

I was so scared and ashamed by that point. My immediate family and my extended family acted as if what they were seeing and I what I was experiencing was normal. No one ever questioned him or me. No one ever asked me if my father was abusing me or doing things to me that made me uncomfortable. No one ever seemed to care what he was doing to me in front of them or how he may have been treating me at home.

There wasn't anyone I dared to trust enough to tell. I once woke up crying. I was terrified my father would tell my mother what we were doing. I was afraid she would hate me for it. When I told him about my nightmare, he reassured me he wouldn't tell *"our secret"* since we both knew mom wouldn't understand. I knew what he was doing to me wasn't right – if something has to be so secretive, then it must be wrong.

I thought about Adam and Eve in the Garden, hiding from God because they were so ashamed of what they had done. I could relate. I too was ashamed.

On a few occasions, my father wanted me to dress up in lingerie and *"model"* for him and my brother. He would make up reasons to send Mom to town – maybe to go buy a pizza for dinner or something else to get her away from the house. After mom left, they would sit and watch me walk around nearly nude. Dad bought a white tank top and cut it off, so it barely covered my breasts. Then, he made me wet it and put it on, so he and my brother could easily see my nipples as I walked around in front of the two of them. My father once made my brother rub lotion on my feet. He said it was good for us to have a *"close"* relationship too.

My father bought various sex toys to use on me, including a nipple chain, which hurt when he put it on me. Sometimes, he would make me wear it under my clothes around other people.

He chose most of my clothes and told me what to wear or not wear. He would often make me dress without wearing panties, even when I would go to a friend's house, so I would think of him while I was gone. After I escaped the situation and decided to share my story, friends and family remarked they had suspected he was sexually involved with me because of the way he acted around me and the way I dressed. But, no one ever said anything while it was happening.

By the time I was 17, my father was talking about making our relationship complete. He would tell me how wonderful it was that I had given my heart to him. He had started saying *"when I was ready"* to fully give my heart to him, I would be ready for sex. His favorite thing to say was how one day he wanted my future husband to thank him for how much he had taught me about how to *"be a good wife."* He always wanted to manipulate me into thinking what he was doing was to help me, not him.

He would often take me out for a drive at night. Then, he would make me get naked in the car while we were riding down the road and tell me no one else could see me since it was dark. He made fun of me and told me not to be so self-conscious when I resisted getting naked.

I wanted to escape the horror that was my life. During the summer when I was 17, I started sneaking out of the house at night. I had discovered how to use the internet to meet people online without my father knowing. But, I wanted to meet them in person too.

I thought my only escape was to meet the internet *"friends"* I was making. I longed for a normal life, but I was forbidden to date at all. I was desperate to meet someone who would rescue me from the hell I was living in at home. I had very little self-worth by that point in my life. I knew sooner or later my father would *"consummate"* our *"relationship."* I was also horribly conflicted, feeling that sex was dirty and shameful while at the same time being encouraged by my dad to embrace and enjoy sex.

I met several different men from the internet. Most would pretend to care for me until they got what they wanted from me which was the same thing my father wanted from me, and then I would never hear from them again.

A few weeks before my 18th birthday, in September of 1998, my father took me on a *"special birthday trip."* We were somewhere in Georgia at a horse show. While we were there, he took me to eat at a Hardee's and then took me to a motel. He started building it up like that night was going to be a really big deal. It was the night he had been waiting so long for. However, it hadn't even gotten dark when he undressed me and climbed on top of me on the bed.

I was unresponsive and crying. He wanted to know why I was being that way. That's not what he wanted or expected. He wanted me to tell him how much I was enjoying it. Everything inside me was screaming for him to stop. When I told him he was hurting me, I had no words to explain he was hurting me much more mentally than he was hurting me physically. I asked him to stop, but he just started saying it would be better the next time.

There would be many *"next times."* None was ever better because he never stopped hurting me.

The first time at the motel, he told me he was surprised at how easy it was to have sex with me. He then convinced himself it was easy because I had been riding horses so much. Of course, he thought I was a virgin and had no idea I had been sneaking out at night and was already having sex with the men I was meeting on the internet as I searched for a way out.

Within weeks of the *"consummation,"* my father gave me a wedding ring. He made me wear it whenever we were alone in public. Several months after the *"special birthday trip"* he informed me my *"education"* wasn't complete. He said I needed to experience more before I was married and committed to one man for the rest of my life.

He had been overruling my objections for many years at that point. He was a master manipulator. I was an 18 year old girl he had been grooming daily since the age of 12. Alone, I was unable to overcome his years of psychological manipulation.

My father told me he would go to hell because of me if I decided I didn't want what he was doing to me. After a few hours of that, I would cave in and agree to whatever it was that he was considering and agree with him that it was God's will. I simply stopped fighting or saying no because every time I did object my father would tell me if I objected it would cause him to sin horribly.

During this phase of the abuse, my father started searching for other people (men and women) to *"help you expand your horizons."* He made me go to the doctor and get a prescription for birth control pills and paid for them each month. He touted religion and the Bible every day and molested me every night.

I was always introduced to the people he found on the internet as his wife. I was only 18 and certainly didn't look old enough to be married to someone who was over 40.

One night in a bar in Birmingham, Alabama, we met a married couple who wanted to have sex with another woman and were willing to let the other man watch. After that meeting, the couple decided not to *"play"* with us, and that was fine with me.

In December of 1998, my father took me to Dollywood in Tennessee where we met an older man. He and my dad had been corresponding via the internet and sex websites. I was told the man was married to a disabled woman who wasn't able to have sex. Dad told me God had provided me for the man, so he wouldn't have to commit adultery.

No one but me seemed to think he was committing adultery if he had sex with me. I was forced to perform oral sex on the man in a storage room behind one of the park attractions. Later, I learned the man worked there. My father had set up the entire situation.

My father also shared me with several different men who were allowed to have sex with me while he watched. He said, *"It's difficult for me to share you, but since you want it so bad, I will do it for you."* I never wanted it, but I didn't feel like I had any options. He decided what I wanted.

When I would tell him I didn't want to do the things he wanted me to do, he would get upset and say, *"You will send me to hell if you don't want to do it."* He would also be sure to tell me, *"I'm trusting you. No one will understand our relationship, so you can't tell anyone. They don't know we are so close and that you want me to do all of these things. Therefore, it's not a sin. Nobody should know how close we are."*

In the spring of 1999, my father took me to Florida. I was still only 18. We met a man there and booked a hotel suite. They took me to McGuire's Irish Pub for dinner. They had dressed me in revealing clothing and called me *"slave"* during the entire meal. After dinner, they took me back to the hotel where they took turns having sex with me. That night, I was tied up, photographed nude, and beaten with a riding crop until bruised all over from my waist to my knees. I was also hung from the ceiling, gagged, and forced to perform various sexual acts. My father and the man kept trying to make me cry out and beg them to stop. But, I wouldn't give in. I thought I was holding on to the one shred of pride I still had by refusing to beg. I obediently participated physically and shut down emotionally in order to deal with what was happening to me. The bruises healed after a few weeks.

I ran away from home several times over the next few months. I was desperate for anyone to save me and keep me from having to return to that horrific life of abuse. Each time I would leave, my father would find me and take me back. He always used emotional blackmail to get me to agree to go back and continue living at home.

At the time, I didn't think it would ever end. I couldn't see a way out. To outsiders, it looked like my life was pretty good. I had my own cell phone, horses, a pool, and I didn't have to work or go to school. I was allowed to do a lot of things as long as I *"asked the right way,"* and those things didn't involve boys or dating.

What I didn't have was privacy, freedom, or even a sense of self-worth. I also didn't have a shred of hope.

Life becomes very dark when you have no hope.

CHAPTER THREE
SOME STRINGS ATTACHED

"We can't gain any momentum moving toward tomorrow if we are dragging the past behind us."

~ Jack Hayford

I met Mack in June of 2000. He was standing outside a nightclub talking with a group of bouncers he knew.

I was supposed to be going bowling in a nearby town with a friend, but instead we traveled for about an hour to get to one of the popular college nightclubs in Auburn, Alabama. I remember changing my clothes on the way and then again on the way back home, so my parents wouldn't wonder what I had really been doing.

I talked to Mack a few hours that night and got to know him a little. We were probably the only two sober people in the club. Several weeks passed before I was able to sneak out and see him again. We emailed and chatted online a few times in between and stayed in contact as much as possible. I started finding ways to sneak in visits whenever I could.

It didn't take long before Mack started suspecting something was strange about my situation. I remember him asking to see my driver's license to confirm my age. He didn't know what I was hiding, but he knew I was hiding something.

Then, one night a couple of months after we started seeing each other, he did what everyone else had avoided doing. He simply asked me if my father was sexually abusing me. I was overwhelmed — no one had ever asked me that question. I wasn't going to lie to him — so I confirmed what he was already thinking. Mack was upset for me and very angry towards my father, but he held me close while I cried. He assured me it wasn't my fault.

He then said he would help me escape from the abusive situation I had been living in for more than seven years. He told me I could stay with him, go to my grandparents' house to live, or we would go to the police. He made it clear it was over, and I wouldn't be going back home to experience any more abuse by my father.

For the first time, I felt like someone cared for me for who I was instead of what I was and what I could do for them sexually. For me, up until that point in my life, the definition of love between a man and a woman was based only on sex.

I had nothing else to compare this new relationship to. Certainly, my parents hadn't modeled anything close to a normal, loving relationship. My father looked down on and tolerated my mother, and I knew they didn't have a whole marriage. I thought they didn't have a true loving relationship because they weren't intimate physically, at least that's what my father had told me.

I also felt incredible freedom for the first time, but then reality came crashing back in on me. I wasn't free yet – I still had to figure out how to end the relationship with my father. I was afraid. For the first time, the future stretched out ahead of me was filled with the unknown.

I was terrified as I thought about what my father would do when I told him I was leaving, and I wouldn't be coming back home. What if he tried to kill himself? How would I live with myself? What if he tried to hurt me, Mack, or Mack's son? I felt he wouldn't let me go without putting up some type of fight.

I decided to ask my closest friend to help me sneak back into my house and get some clothes. I shared the truth with her, and she too had suspected it all along. My plan worked. We didn't even have to confront my father at all. I believe God sent angels to protect me that day. I certainly felt protected like never before. My friend also called my parents after I was safely back with Mack and simply told them I would never be coming home.

A few weeks after my daring escape, my mom made an appearance at Mack's home where I had decided to live. They had tracked his phone number from my cell phone records to find his name and address. She stood outside and shouted until I finally decided to let her in.

I didn't tell her anything, even though she cried and pleaded with me to tell her why I had suddenly left home. She visited me once a week for about three more weeks. Each time she came, she would bring me something from home and take me out to eat, so we could talk. I did want her to bring my dog Solomon, but Mack and I had no room for a large dog. I knew I wouldn't be able to keep him. I was later told my father had shot and killed him.

After lunch on her third visit, she sat with me in the living room and begged one more time for me to talk to her about why I had left. She promised she would always love me. I hoped it was true and broke down crying as I finally told her dad had been sexually abusing me for years.

After sobbing for a few minutes, I reached out to hug her, but she pushed me away. I didn't feel loved by her as she had just promised to do moments before. She first said I was making it all up, and I was mentally unstable. She said she had always been afraid I was mentally sick, and I would have to be treated for having delusions. I was shocked and hurt beyond words. I told her to leave and not to come back.

However, she returned again a week later. There was a new hardness in her. She didn't bring me anything from home, and I wouldn't go anywhere with her to eat like I had done before. She started our visit by saying she had asked my father if I was telling the truth, and he admitted that some of what I had shared with her was true. It was all true.

My mother said I had tempted him and caused him to sin. She said it was my fault he had lusted after me, and I should not have caused him to sin. She told me I was going to hell for what I had done and for bringing shame to our family. I haven't talked to her since that day 17 years ago in October of 2000.

My father called me on my birthday, October 8, 2000, a month after I had left. At first, I wouldn't talk to him. Mack answered and talked to him for a while before asking me if I was sure I wanted to talk to him at all. I didn't know it at the time, but Mack confronted him and told him some of the things I had told him my father had done to me. Mack later told me my dad didn't deny it or say I was lying. He simply said, *"She's finally found someone she trusts hasn't she."*

I accepted the phone from Mack and just sobbed, while my father tried one more time to get me to come home. He kept telling me it was my last chance for salvation and my last hope of making it to heaven – I had to come back home and *"make it right"* he said.

While on the phone, I told my mother and father one last time to leave me alone. I said if they left me alone, I wouldn't go to the police about what he had done to me. I didn't know it then, but Mack had also told my father if he contacted me again after that day, he would tell my story to the police immediately whether I wanted him to or not. Mack had made it clear to my father that the choice of what was going to happen to him going forward was up to him.

The days of him manipulating, controlling, and abusing me were over.

I didn't want to press charges then because I didn't think I could face the investigation and the process of having everything I was so ashamed of brought out publicly. I had very little self-confidence, self-worth, and self-respect as it was. All I wanted was my freedom, to be loved, and to be left alone.

A few weeks after leaving, I was able to share with both sets of my Grandparents why I had left home and why I would not be going back. I didn't want to tell them, but I realized they needed to know.

My parents were furious with me for telling my grandparents the truth. They wanted my grandparents to choose not to talk to me, since I was *"such a sinner."* My grandparents, on both sides, supported me and refused to cut me off. My parents eventually moved to a different state and took my brother with them.

Mack encouraged me to take my time finding a job and to consider going to college before going to work, but I wanted my own money. I never wanted to be without options again. I didn't want to be restricted in regard to where I could go or where I lived, and I knew getting a job was the first step toward becoming an independent woman.

I immediately hit my first roadblock. Since I had been homeschooled, I didn't have a high school diploma from a recognized or state approved school. I knew that would limit my job search.

The only job I could find was working as a waitress. It was hard work, but I was glad to do it and proud of myself. For the first time in my life, I was earning my own money. My first paycheck was a joke. I was making $2.13 an hour plus tips. All the tips I reported were deducted back off my paycheck for taxes. But, it didn't matter how small my check was because it was mine. Starting then, I would always have cash in my pocket. I could buy something without having to ask for money from others.

I had started making some important decisions on my own. I was in control. I was responsible.

Mack and I got engaged several months after we met and were married about a year later. We agreed to wait to marry until I was 21, so I would have more than a year of freedom behind me after leaving home to be sure I was making the right decision.

I tried to put the abuse behind me and look forward. I didn't want to talk about my parents, what my father had done to me, or how I was coping with it. I wanted to forget it and move on, not realizing I was creating my own sort of prison by allowing it to control me from within.

I am very blessed to have Mack and couldn't help feeling like he got more than he bargained for. I certainly came with strings attached in the form of my past and the emotional difficulties I would face while overcoming it. Even today, I still have nightmares and wake up crying from dreams where I find myself back in my father's house desperate to escape.

It takes a strong man to be able to rescue a broken woman and to give her the time, space, and support to truly become the woman she has the potential of becoming. Mack did everything he could for me to encourage and support me, all while knowing I could very well have started to heal and decided he wasn't the right man for me. He knew that and told me it would be okay. He wanted what was best for me even if what was best for me didn't include him.

I realized after getting my first paycheck I needed to go to college if I wanted to find a better job. No one would hire me for much more than waitressing without skills, experience, and a high school diploma or GED. After our wedding, I started spending my nights studying and passed the GED exam on the first try. I started looking for another job and also began taking classes at a community college.

There were quite a few obstacles along the way, but the biggest one was myself. I had extremely poor people skills as you can imagine considering the controlling and manipulative environment I had been trapped in. I wasn't shy but lacked confidence, skills, and experience in connecting with people. I never knew what to say or do around strangers, and social situations terrified me. I was sure I would commit some social blunder. I would never initiate a conversation because I didn't know how to get started or where to go with it if I did.

I also felt people were looking down on me because I was young and waiting tables. You see the worst and the best side of people relative to how they view and treat those they feel can do nothing for them.

Mack had a great job and an associate degree at the time. Most of my new stepson's friends had parents who were nurses, lawyers, realtors, or didn't work at all. There were only a few instances where someone said or did something insensitive, but I took every one to heart because I lacked self-confidence and security in who I was at the time. I traveled a long way to get to where I am today.

Determined not to let my circumstances hold me back, I set my sights high. I wanted to work at the local hospital on the administrative side and decided I wanted to earn my MBA by the time I was 30.

I was willing to work hard, and that took me a long way. I was willing to learn, and that took me even further. I made my share of mistakes but always pushed forward.

To supplement my income, I waited tables off and on in a couple of different restaurants until 2007. I worked my way up through several medical positions in various medical offices and received several promotions along the way. I finally landed my dream job working at the hospital in the compliance department. I continued to take college classes, sometimes while working two jobs and seven days a week. Eventually, I climbed all the way up to Director of Regulatory Affairs and Compliance for the entire hospital.

I also started teaching many different types of group fitness classes each week, completed several full marathons, and learned to mountain bike where I won the Alabama and Georgia State Championships in my class in 2011 and 2012. I let go of some limiting beliefs.

Growing up, my father had made fun of my attempts to do anything athletic other than riding horses, and I believed what he said. No longer under his control and manipulation, I was proving him wrong every chance I got. I believed it was possible. Then, I made it happen.

In 2012, I graduated from Auburn University of Montgomery with a 4.0 cumulative GPA which I maintained starting from community college all the way to graduating with my MBA. Mack and only a few other close family members and friends knew just how far I had come. In that moment, it wasn't that I was proud of the degree – but I was proud of the woman I had become while earning it. I now had confidence. I now had self-esteem. I now had my own life.

Life was good, and my future was only getting brighter.

CHAPTER FOUR
A DEFINING MOMENT

"It is in the moments of decision that your destiny is shaped."

~ Tony Robbins

In February 2013, I was sitting in a conference room with hundreds of other people when Les Brown took the stage. I didn't even know who he was at the time. He spoke for a couple of hours, but I only remember one sentence: *"You have a story to tell. Someone needs to hear your story, and only you can help that person."*

Sitting in the audience, I was stunned. Was Les talking to me? Surely not. I knew I had a story to tell, but I didn't want to tell it. I wasn't sure I could tell it. In fact, I had spent 13 years trying very hard to avoid mentioning my past.

What would people think if they knew what my father, and the men he shared me with, had done to me? What would people think if I told them where I came from and what I had experienced? What would people think if they found out what my father had really been doing to me all of those nights when he *"tucked me in?"* How could I face anyone who knew there might still be nude pictures of me on the internet?

I immediately decided not to think about it. Les Brown didn't know me, and he certainly didn't know my story. I didn't think anyone needed to know my story. Knowing the terrible circumstances of my past, my guilt, my shame, and my fear wouldn't help anyone.

At the time, Mack and I were in Orlando for a leadership conference, and Les Brown was one of the speakers at the event. Mack had been working very successfully as a Lean Manufacturing consultant for about four years when he decided to rebrand his business around leadership development. Excited about the possibilities, he wanted me to attend the conference in

Orlando with him.

I wasn't quite as excited as Mack. I was very happy and content in my role as Director of Regulatory Affairs and Compliance at the hospital. I had a great job at a great organization, and I had a great boss whom I adored. I had worked hard to become very successful in my career and had gone to college for many years to prepare for it. I agreed to attend the conference with Mack because he insisted it would help me advance my career.

The conference had been life changing for me in the few days before I heard Les Brown speak. It opened my eyes to an entirely new set of possibilities beyond working at the hospital for the rest of my career as I had planned. I became excited about the possibilities of becoming a leadership coach, trainer, and speaker as long as I didn't have to talk about myself. Ignoring my protests that we shouldn't spend any more money, Mack registered both of us on the spot and paid for us to attend an upcoming speaker training seminar with Les Brown six months later in August.

Returning home from the February conference, I resolved to focus my energy on exploring the possibilities of coaching, speaking, and training on leadership development. I also resolved to forget Les Brown's words about helping someone else by sharing my story.

However, they were burned into my heart. I had always wanted to help people which is why I went into healthcare. My experiences in patient care, and even later on the administrative side of healthcare, were very fulfilling because I knew I was helping others.

I was no longer the shy, scared, broken girl who had left home at 19 to escape years of sexual, emotional, psychological, and physical abuse. When I had left home 13 years before, the only possessions I had in the world were a few pillowcases and one duffle bag stuffed with clothes. The people I worked with at the hospital and those who saw me speak on stage at the statewide revenue integrity committee meetings would have never believed where I had come from. They really had no idea.

I now had responsibilities for thousands of organizational compliance policies, licensure for hundreds of healthcare providers, and oversight for millions of dollars in Medicare insurance filing appeals. Mack and I had three very nice cars, a nice house with a hot tub and a pool, and we vacationed in Hawaii the year before. Life was good for us.

We had also helped form a community non-profit mountain biking organization and had spent thousands of hours volunteering to make sure it was a success. Mack served as the founding president of the organization. And as founding secretary, I had written a grant application that resulted in the organization receiving a $100,000 grant to improve the mountain biking trails in the local state park.

We had been very successful. But, we were beginning to leverage the success we had achieved for ourselves in an effort to make a significant positive impact in the lives of others.

After the initial conference in February, I spent the next six months learning all I could. We rebranded Mack's consulting business and invested over $15,000 with a consulting firm to help us with marketing and PR. That turned out to be a mistake because we didn't get any real return on our investment. What we didn't know and what we did wrong could fill a book, but we were willing to try, learn, and try again. We only fail if we quit trying. We have never quit trying and will always be learning.

We went to Guatemala with John Maxwell and 150

other coaches in June 2013 to train 20,000 leaders on leadership and personal growth principles.

While all of this was happening, I continued to feel a gentle nudge from God to share my story.

I've always had a contrary, some may say stubborn, streak, and perhaps that served me well in overcoming the years of abuse. But, it doesn't help when God calls you to do something, and you refuse. Thankfully, He didn't have to send a whale my way to convince me.

In August 2013, Mack and I returned to Orlando for the Les Brown speaker training. During the two day training event, each one of the 200 or so in attendance was required to create and deliver a scripted one minute speech. There would be three rounds of judging where ultimately the five best speakers were selected. Those five winners would be offered an opportunity to share the stage with Les Brown at one of his future events. I had been struggling with the decision to share my story for six months. I knew it was now or never.

As I rehearsed the night before the conference, I didn't share with anyone what the topic of my one minute speech would be. I wasn't sure I could go through with it, and I needed to work through that myself without the (well-meant) encouragement from others which would put additional pressure on me.

I couldn't even say the words out loud to myself in private. Fighting the urge to be physically sick, I broke down crying in the ladies' room just before walking in to the conference. The bonds of shame and fear, along with having a false sense of guilt, had been holding me captive for more than 20 years. The thought of breaking my silence publicly was almost too much for me to contemplate.

In the ladies' room, I repaired my mascara and simply

prayed, *"God, I can't do this. Lord, if this is your will, give me the strength."* That was the moment I truly began my *relationship* with God. I had been raised believing in God and Jesus. However, until that moment, I had not experienced the comfort and strength of a relationship with Him. It didn't happen until I was willing to surrender my own agenda and become obedient to His.

The strength to share my story came from something much greater than me.

At the end of that long day, it didn't matter to me if I had won the contest or not. I had won a much greater victory in my heart when I told the world I wasn't going to be ashamed of what had happened to me any longer. And, in saying that out loud to a room full of people, I proved it. As my friend Chawanis Ash said, *"Although it may be difficult to face the ugly pain of our past, we cannot conquer what we are not willing to confront."*

For the first time, I was willing to publicly confront my past, and therefore, I was positioned to conquer it.

The response from the audience after my speech was overwhelming. 200 other speakers, all competing for the same opportunity I was, gave me a standing ovation. Every person I passed on the way back to my seat gave me a high-five, a hug, or a handshake.

As it turns out, I was one of the five winners selected and was invited to share the stage with Les Brown in Los Angeles a few months later.

It was a defining moment in my life. I knew the time had come to make an even bigger decision. I had a successful career, but I couldn't deny the calling God had just placed on my life. 10 days after giving what turned out to be a 47 second version of my story, I decided to walk away from a career to follow my calling.

CHAPTER FIVE
THE REST OF THE STORY

"I can be changed by what happens to me, but I refuse to be reduced by it."

~ Maya Angelou

January 3, 2014 was my last day in the corporate world. I withdrew my retirement savings, updated my LinkedIn profile, and started writing a book. I had no idea how I was going to become a motivational speaker, I simply knew I was called to do it. God doesn't (usually) provide us with a roadmap on how to get to where He wants us to be when He gives us a calling. But, He does equip us for the journey He wants us to take.

I also understand *"...to whom much is given, from him much will be required..."* (Luke 12:48) What we do with the gifts, experiences, talents, abilities, and resources He gives us is up to us. I consider it a stewardship.

I had the misconception that if I simply started speaking about my story event planners would flock to book me to speak at their events.

It didn't go exactly like I thought it would.

Mack and I went to Los Angeles in January 2014 after I received my formal invitation from Les Brown. When we got there, he actually invited both of us to share the stage with him. We were privileged to speak at his event and to be personally coached and mentored by him too. It was a tremendous experience for us. I was also selected to speak on stage at John Maxwell's International Certification events three different times. I considered it a privilege each time. But, none of those experiences set us up for instant success as speakers and trainers.

Mack and I worked very hard those first few years. It certainly required many sacrifices on our part. We downsized our cars for several years, so we could invest more money in our business. We sold the home in

Auburn, Alabama that we loved dearly and moved to the Atlanta, Georgia area, so we would be close to a major airport and a large city. We significantly modified our lifestyle and cut out unnecessary spending. When your dream is worth pursuing, the sacrifices come easy.

And, when you love what you do, it's not really work. As Albert Schweltzer said, *"Success is not the key to happiness. Happiness is the key to success. If you love what you are doing, you will be successful."* It's still not unusual for us to work every day, on the weekends, and even during the holidays. But, we also have the flexibility to take off mid-week and go hiking or do whatever we want to do whenever we want to do it. We only do what we want to do when we want to do it. Life is good.

I am often asked, *"How did you actually start speaking?"* There were many mistakes along the way, but the short answer is, *"Be a speaker, and start doing the things speakers do."* If you do the work, the rest will happen when it's supposed to happen. It's not easy. Like any goal worth working for, it takes time, effort, energy, focus, dedication, and the willpower to say *"no"* to the things that will hold you back or slow you down.

When I started speaking, I tried everything I could think of to get more opportunities to speak. Some ideas were good – some were not so good. I once contacted every single Kiwanis club in the state and offered to speak at their meetings. More than one club took me up on my offer. Mack and I drove more than two hours one way to speak (unpaid) for 20 minutes at a breakfast meeting at one of the clubs and then turned around and drove back home.

Speakers speak. Paid. Unpaid. Close to home. Far away from home. At big events. At small events.

Many people I meet and talk to would like to become

a professional speaker. The question they must answer for themselves is not, *"Do I want to become a speaker?"* but rather, *"Am I willing to put in the work that's required to become a successful speaker?"*

Writing books has certainly helped me, both in discovering how to tell my story and in reaching more people with my message. Mack and I have published 20 books on leadership development and personal growth. There are people whom I have never met who send me messages and share with me the impact my books have had on them. It's very humbling and rewarding to receive these messages. Knowing I've helped make one person's journey easier gives meaning and value to my own journey and makes it all worth it.

Today, Mack and I are speaking regularly together on leadership development and personal growth topics such as communication, change, leadership, resilience, time management, transformation, and much more at various types of events such as: conferences, seminars, retreats, professional associations, workshops, church groups, colleges, high schools, corporate groups, and more.

I also coach a select group of clients who want to learn how to effectively tell, deliver, and brand their own story – it's very rewarding to share many of the lessons I've learned along the way and accelerate someone else's journey toward success.

There aren't any shortcuts. You must travel the path that must be traveled. However, you can definitely go slower or go faster down that path. I enjoy helping others go faster. I think the biggest lesson I've learned is to build relationships and to focus on becoming more valuable instead of focusing on becoming more successful.

Albert Einstein said, *"Try not to become a man of success, but rather try to become a man of value."* When you are providing value, people will value you. Valuable people are valued by people.

Since 2014, Mack and I have been very blessed with many opportunities in the work we do. We were invited to tour San Quentin Prison in California after speaking to a large group of prison wardens from around the country. We spent several hours inside of San Quentin with the wardens and the inmates who were leading the tour. It was truly an amazing experience.

We've also recently been to Delaware where I was invited to speak at the TEDx Wilmington Women's Conference. We have served a number of Fortune 500 companies and several government agencies by providing various leadership development programs. We've spoken to high school students and high level business leaders across many different industries and with many other people at all levels in between.

I'm living proof that what happens to us in life is not what's most important. What's most important is what we do and who we become as result of what happened to us. What matters is the rest of our story – and it's not written yet. We writeyour story every day, one choice and decision at a time.

My story isn't over yet. Until October 2016, my father had done as we had asked and left us alone. I had also done as I had promised and not reported the seven years of sexual, physical, and psychological abuse he had put me through. And, it would have been far easier for me if he had continued to stay out of our lives as he had done the previous 16 years. But, we seldom get what we want in life.

In October 2016, my father started sending letters to my Grandparents to harass them. He stated they needed to forget me or pretend I didn't exist, so they could establish a relationship with him again. He didn't accept responsibility for what he did to me. He also didn't offer any apologies for what he did to me or how he treated our entire family in the past. He inserted himself back into our lives by attempting to manipulate my family members to choose – him or me.

On October 14, 2016, within 24 hours of learning my father had re-entered my life, I called the authorities, scheduled an appointment, and filed a report against him for what he did to me. He was indicted by a grand jury and officially offered a plea deal on November 21, 2017. However, he continued to avoid taking responsibility for what he did to me and rejected the deal.

As I write these words, we are waiting for a trial date to be set. I'm sure walking into a courtroom and testifying will be the most difficult thing I've ever done. It's going to be a very public exposure of the very personal details I was so ashamed of for so long.

On top of the stress I'm experiencing, it's painful to see my family, grandparents, brother, aunts, etc. dragged through this process too. However, I know there's only one person responsible for all of this pain. It's not me. It's my father who chose to do what he did to me.

We all would have preferred to move on and leave the past in the past, but my father chose to come back into our lives. The consequences of his recent actions mean he will also now face the consequences for the choices he made many years ago. We can all choose our actions, but we don't get to choose the consequences that flow from those actions. Natural laws and principles will determine the consequences of our actions. They always have, and they always will.

I'm not happy or glad there will be a trial. However, I'm prepared. I'm ready to do what must be done. I am not the isolated, helpless, manipulated, and controlled young girl my father spent seven years grooming me to be. That young girl moved out when I did. She doesn't live here anymore.

Today, I am a free, strong, confident, proud, courageous woman who is standing on the shoulders of thousands of men and women who now support me and believe in me. I'm grateful for them all. They give me strength and courage.

PART II:
A BLUEPRINT FOR BRIDGE BUILDING

CHAPTER SIX
RESPOND PROACTIVELY

"We build too many walls and not enough bridges."

~ Isaac Newton

Resilience is when we learn to build a bridge out of the past, instead of building a wall around it. Far too often, we wall up the pain of the past, thinking we are protecting ourselves from it. But, when we close off the pain from the past, we also numb the joy of the present. We can't numb one emotion without numbing another. And, pretending the pain isn't there doesn't make it go away. To truly overcome something in our past, we must be willing to build a bridge out of our past and into our future.

I've created a simple blueprint for building these bridges using the acronym RISE, which means we must *"Respond Proactively, Identify Accurately, Step Forward Consistently, and Experience Joy."* Although I couldn't articulate this until many years after leaving my parents' home, these are the steps that have allowed me to overcome adversity in my life, both past and present.

You can use this blueprint to build your own bridges. Building bridges doesn't mean your past won't still be painful, or your present won't be difficult. It simply means you have a new skillset that, when applied, will allow you to create the life you want.

The first step is to *"Respond Proactively."*

The dictionary defines *"proactive"* as an adjective meaning, *"Serving to prepare for, intervene in, or control an expected occurrence or situation, especially a negative or difficult one; anticipatory."* (*www.Dictionary.com/Proactive retrieved November 24, 2017*)

Stephen R. Covey defined proactive as *"choosing the response you will have to any stimulus."* To be proactive, you choose your response to any situation or stimulus in life, expected or not. If you fail to choose, a choice in itself, you will become reactive to the stimulus and simply respond based on the emotions of the moment.

As Scott Peck said, *"...There are indeed oppressive forces at work within the world. We have, however, the freedom to choose every step of the way the manner in which we are going to respond to and deal with these forces."*

For me, responding proactively to the past and to the present requires two different approaches.

R – Respond Proactively: To Past Circumstances

Proactive and reactive people alike are affected by what happens in life. However, proactive people choose *how* they are affected by what happens. They choose *how* the little things and the big things that have happened to them during their life will affect them.

We have the ability and the responsibility to look back at a situation or something that has happened in our lives, to reflect on it, and to consciously choose *how* to view the experience. We will choose to respond either positively or negatively.

Proactive people always choose to discover, uncover, and leverage the positive in any situation. Regardless of how painful, difficult, hard, or awful the experience may have been, proactive people always make a decision to view it in a positive light.

To a reactive person, this seems counterintuitive. *"There is no way I can view the death of my child as something positive,"* a grieving mother may think. Yet, I know one such mother who did exactly that. In doing so, she has given additional meaning to her daughter's life by turning the story of her battle with cancer into an incredibly inspiring book that delivers hope to many others.

Those who don't understand the concept of being proactive often say to me, *"How can you view what your father did to you in a positive way? There is no way I could view seven years of horrible sexual and psychological abuse as something positive."*

I simply choose to apply the principle of being proactive. I choose to view the negative things that happened in a positive way. My father controlled me and abused me physically and emotionally for years, but he cannot, and never could, control my freedom to choose how it affected me. Therefore, I choose to be better because of it instead of bitter about it. My past doesn't define the woman I am today. Only I can do that. Your past doesn't define you either. Only you can do that.

R – Respond Proactively: To Present Circumstances

For me, responding proactively to present stimulus and circumstances is more of a challenge because I don't have the time to reflect, think, and carefully decide how it is affecting me. Many things that happen in life require an instant response, or lack of response, in the moment. It often feels more emotional because it feels more immediate.

Responding proactively in the moment means you realize you can't control everything that is happening or that is about to happen. But, you can always control your response to what has just happened or what is still happening.

When you don't like what has happened, you can choose your attitude and response to the situation and your circumstances. I'm training for a marathon and had a nine mile training run scheduled this morning. When I awoke, it was raining and continued to drizzle rain most of the morning which made my nine mile run very uncomfortable. In fact, the conditions were downright miserable.

I couldn't control the conditions. But, I could control my response to the conditions. So, I ran anyway. With soggy shoes, wet clothes, and a smile. External circumstances do not dictate how I feel inside. Only I can do that. Proactive people carry their weather within.

When someone says something you don't like, you have the freedom to choose to respond reactively from a position of anger or hurt in the moment. Most often, we end up regretting these emotionally charged responses later.

However, you also have the freedom to choose to respond to the same situation in a careful and intentional proactive way that allows you to harness and suppress the emotion of the moment. Responding without being angry or hurt allows you to respond based on the values you truly care about. Most often, choosing a proactive response based on internalized values produces a far better outcome than choosing a reactive response that is based on your feelings and the emotions of the moment.

Responding proactively means you maintain control in spite of your feelings. Other people cannot dictate how you feel on the inside. They can't make you hurt, upset, frustrated, mad, or sad. They can't make you happy, joyful, excited, or delighted. You are the only one who can determine how you feel on the inside. If you don't choose to become responsible, you have chosen to be irresponsible.

Dr. Edith Eger stated, *"Our painful experiences aren't a liability, they're a gift. They give us perspective and meaning, an opportunity to find our unique purpose and our strength."* It is not what happens to us that determines how we feel. The things that happen to us only influence us. They do not determine us. It is our response to what happens to us that determines how we feel. Things only become painful when we choose to see them in a painful, reactive way.

Much like you must continually exercise to maintain your physical health, you must also continually practice being proactive to maintain positive mental health. Choosing to be proactive isn't always easy. However, it is always worth it. The more you *choose* to be proactive, the easier it becomes to *be* proactive.

Perhaps, you may eventually master the art of becoming proactive to all situations and to every stimulus in life. It's possible. I haven't arrived yet, but I work to improve and strengthen my proactive *"mind muscles"* every day.

Sonya Friedman said it best, *"You have control over three things: what you think, what you say, and how you behave. To make a change in your life, you must recognize these gifts are the most powerful tools you possess in shaping the form of your life."*

CHAPTER SEVEN
IDENTIFY ACCURATELY

"Short or long term, the clearer we can see what we are setting out to achieve, the more likely we are to achieve it."

~ Simon Sinek

Once you choose to *"Respond Proactively,"* the second step is to *"Identify Accurately."* Far too often when we aren't being intentional, we end up wasting our precious time and energy on things we don't really want or need in our lives. Living life on purpose requires us to be intentional. The first step toward becoming intentional is to identify what we are going to be intentional about. It's unfortunate that our natural *"Fight, Flight, or Freeze"* responses often deter us from using our most valuable resource: our mind.

George Bernard Shaw stated it well, *"The people who get on in this world are the people who get up and look for the circumstances they want, and if they can't find them, make them."*

I – Identify Accurately: Where are you? Where do you want to go? How will you get there?

If we don't know where we are or where we're going, how will we know when we reach our destination? How will we determine if we're moving in the right direction? Or worse, will we even know or care which direction we are heading? Truthfully, until we know where we want to go, it doesn't really matter where we are or which way we're heading.

Resilient people identify where they want to go, where they are, and then identify the steps they must take in order to move from where they are to where they want to be.

I started my career working as a waitress in a pizza restaurant making $2.13 an hour plus tips. My first paycheck was more than a paycheck, it was also a reality check.

Even when working full-time, any tips I earned were then deducted from my $2.13 an hour paycheck. As a result, some of my paychecks totaled less than $20.00 after taxes for two weeks of hard work.

At that time, I wasn't really sure what my dream job was, but I did realize it wouldn't come looking for me. I was going to have to go looking for it.

Regardless of where you have come from and where you are now, you do not have to stay there.

Most often, it's not our physical circumstances that keep us stuck. It's our emotional circumstances that do all the damage. As Daniel Goleman said, *"Self-awareness - recognizing a feeling as it happens - is the keystone of emotional intelligence."*

Self-awareness is also the key to understanding when we're moving in the right direction. The biggest obstacle to achieving anything in our lives is the false assumption that we cannot achieve what we want to achieve. Then, based on those false beliefs, we create our reality.

Increasing your self-awareness isn't easy. It requires you to do the difficult work of determining your values, reflecting on them, and then evaluating them in order to determine how they have influenced your thoughts, decisions, choices, actions, consequences, and ultimately, how they have created your current circumstances.

You should do this exercise intentionally for all four dimensions of your life: Physical, Relational, Emotional, and Spiritual. Until you are able to accurately identify where you are and where you want to be, you won't be able to figure out how to get there.

In the physical dimension of your life, take a few moments and honestly reflect on where you are in terms of physical health and wellness. Do you exercise regularly? Are you healthy? Do you have bad health habits that are taking years off of your life?

Then, reflect on where you want to be and what you should start doing differently to reach your goal. I don't mean imagine a picture perfect body like you saw on the cover of a magazine. I do mean truly reflect on what your *"ideal physical healthy state"* should be and what that would look like for *you* compared to *where you actually are today.*

The concept is that once you honestly know where you are now and where you truly want to be, you have identified the gap and can stop making excuses and start accepting responsibility for closing that gap.

Where are you in terms of your relational life? Do you have positive relationships with people who support you? Are there harmful, toxic, or negative relationships that you need to terminate? Most often, the people closest to us are the ones holding us back the most because they have the most influence in our lives.

The most powerful example from my life was my father and mother. They held me back more than anyone else ever has or will. They should have been supporting me the most, but they chose not to support me at all. People who aren't close to us have little, if any, influence in our lives. Be careful, be intentional, and evaluate those who are closest to you.

Sometimes, we need to end or change relationships with one or more of those who are closest to us. It doesn't necessarily mean the people are bad. It does mean it's a relationship that doesn't support us, our growth, and our goals.

I was on a coaching call recently with one of my clients. She determined she wanted to build more relationships. To help raise her self-awareness about what that meant, I encouraged and questioned her, *"That's great! But, what kind of relationships do you want to create and with whom?"*

Where are you in terms of your emotional life? Are you happy? Are you sad? Is your life full of joy? Is your life full of drama? Are you growing? Are you slowing? Are you fulfilled? Are you drained? What thoughts are you having about your life? What thoughts should you be having? As James Allen remarked, *"The outer word of circumstance shapes itself to the inner world of thought."*

Where are you in your spiritual life? Do you make time for reflection, prayer, or meditation? Is there balance and harmony in your life? Is there chaos in your life? Are you in alignment with why you are here? Is your relationship with God strong?

Once you *Identify Accurately* what success looks like, you will be positioned to know what must be done to convert that image of success in your mind into a reality in your life. For example, if you want to run a marathon, you need to honestly identify what your current physical state is. Assuming it's physically possible for you to run, then you need to identify what is required of you to achieve that goal. Next, identify the healthy choices a person who wants to run a marathon will make such as: eating nutritiously, resting and sleeping diligently, and training hard consistently and methodically.

Knowing what to do is no longer an issue. Now, you must act. You can and must make it happen, or it's not going to happen. No one can do it for you but you.

The question you must now answer is, *"Am I truly willing to commit to those choices?"* Do it, and you will reach your goal. Don't do it, and you won't. It's really that simple. But, it's not that easy.

CHAPTER EIGHT
STEP FORWARD CONSISTENTLY

"Too often, we want to feel our way into action, when instead we need to act our way into feeling."

~ John C. Maxwell

Once you have identified the right path and a way forward, the third step is to MOVE down the path! It's time to *"Step Forward Consistently"* in order to reach your goal. Stop waiting until tomorrow, next week, next year, or until the weather, time, or situation is perfect.

In the words of Zig Ziglar, *"You don't have to be great to start, but you have to start to be great."* Start, and you'll be on your way to great. But, you can't stop. You're either moving forward or backward. You're never standing still because the world is constantly in motion around you.

If a journey of a thousand miles begins with a single step, take that single step but don't stop there. Take another and another. As Mack says, *"When you have a mountain to climb, don't focus on the mountain. Focus on the moment. Conquer enough moments, and you will eventually conquer the mountain."*

S – Step Forward Consistently: Take Action and Keep Moving

Whether it's overcoming adversity or achieving any goal in life, moving forward, even if it's only one inch at a time, is the key to success.

Jim Rohn once said, *"Success is nothing more than a few simple disciplines, practiced every day."*

When looking at a big goal, break it down into small steps. Take the first step. Then, tomorrow you can take the second step. And, just keep going.

In 2011, Mack and I started racing mountain bikes, the kind you pedal. And, we were pedaling them through the woods on unpaved, rough, rocky, root covered dirt trails. We had started riding for recreation in 2009. For someone who is not naturally gifted as an athlete, it was challenging to simply ride a mountain bike on the trails, much less compete at a fast race pace.

I was terrified of crashing and getting hurt and had been from the start. When we first started riding, we rode around town, so I could learn the basics. The curbs along the sidewalks always gave me trouble. I would get off my bike and lift it on or off the curb when transitioning to or from the street rather than trying to ride up and over the curb or off of it like I do now.

When I decided to start riding through the woods, I was so far outside my comfort zone, that I wasn't even on the same map. There were many things that were much more challenging than curbs. Every trail was full of these challenges, and each challenge was unique and different from the last. Plus, the difficulty level was multiplied whenever the trail was wet.

We enjoyed the opportunity to get outside and exercise by mountain biking on many different trails, but I didn't like to go too fast. I always fell behind when we rode. I took my time navigating through the trails and frequently got off to push my bike around difficult sections, rocks, roots, or steep hills. And still, I had my share of crashes, bruises, cuts, and scrapes. Every bike ride left me exhausted mentally and physically, and frequently frustrated because of my lack of skills.

When Mack signed us up for the first race, I expected him to do well, but thought I had zero chance of being competitive.

That first race day was literally a mess. It rained heavily for hours before the race started, and the trail was muddy and very slippery. By the time my group started, the expert and advanced riders had churned many laps, turning the mud on the trail into a thick, slippery goop.

It was ugly. I slipped, slid, and crashed my way through my nine mile lap to the finish line.

I couldn't believe it when I won.

It was the beginning of two years of competing seriously, and I won four state championships in my division during that two year time period. Then, that season of our lives passed. And, I moved on to other things and new challenges.

Mountain biking taught me what I lacked in skill or ability, I could make up for with determination and sheer perseverance.

Life is almost always like that too. What often prevents our success is not that we aren't capable of reaching our goal, it's that we quit trying and give up before we reach our goal. It's too easy to give up and make excuses, especially when those around us will agree with us and help us make the excuses.

You can find an excuse, or you can find a way. Whatever you look for, you will find. If you settle for an excuse, you will never find a way. Og Mandino said, *"Failure will never overtake me if my determination to succeed is strong enough."*

I knew I was setting a big goal when I started college. I wanted to go all the way, and I wasn't even sure exactly what I meant when I said that. However, I did know it would take years. Many people with a past similar to mine would have never even tried. I didn't even have a GED or high school diploma, and I had never stepped foot in a classroom or school with other people.

But, what got me to that graduation ceremony more than 10 years later where I received my Master's Degree in Business Administration with a career 4.0 GPA was focusing on one test, one class, and one semester at a time.

I didn't get discouraged when I didn't ace a test, I became more determined to study harder and make up the difference. I made a "D" on an anatomy exam one time because I didn't prepare well enough. I knew I was in trouble the moment I started the test. I was working in an orthopedic clinic at the time and identifying bones should have been easy for me since I worked with them all day every day. But, they looked quite different individually and disconnected instead of being connected in the form of a skeleton as I was used to seeing them.

My teacher told me it would be nearly impossible to get an "A" in the class after that because I would have to make 95 or better on the remaining three exams. She didn't believe in extra credit or make up work either, so there were no other options. My only hope for an "A" was scoring almost 100 on every remaining test. I didn't listen to how hard it was going to be, I listened to the fact that it was possible, and I focused on that. Then, I made it happen. I earned my "A" in that class.

If you want to conquer the challenge, conquer the moment. Conquer the moments, and the mission will take care of itself.

Resilience is having the relentless determination to keep going when you become lost, when you are forced to take a detour, or when you hit a roadblock.

It's easy to decide to change something. What determines success is having the discipline to actually make the change after you decide to do it. "Deciding to do" and "actually doing" are two very different things.

CHAPTER NINE
EXPERIENCE JOY

"Most people live either in their memories of the past or their hopes for the future. Few live in the present."

~ Ricardo Semler

The fourth step is to *"Experience Joy."* Some of you may be thinking, *"That's not a step."* But, it is. Because we can be just as intentional about experiencing joy as we can about being proactive, intentional, and disciplined.

E – Experience Joy

An abundant, joyful life is not just for some people. It's for anyone with the integrity, strength, desire, and the courage to claim it.

Life is meant to be lived. A phrase in my favorite book reminds us that we should, *"...have life, and have it **more abundantly.**"*

Abundance is about experiencing joy. If you aren't experiencing joy and abundance, you are merely surviving, not thriving. Choosing to become resilient means you stop surviving, and start thriving.

Joy isn't a product of our circumstances. It's not just an emotion we can feel. It's a choice we must make. Choose joy. Choosing joy is the ultimate expression of being proactive. Our happiness in life isn't dependent on external conditions. Certainly, it might be easier to be joyful when things are going well. But, it's not impossible to be joyful when they aren't.

So many people fail to actually live life and end up simply going through the motions. Oprah Winfrey advised, *"My number one spiritual practice is trying to live in the moment...to resist projecting into the future, or lamenting past mistakes...to feel the real power of now. That, my friends, is the secret to a joyful life."*

The key to understanding this step is understanding the difference between joy and pleasure.

Pleasure is a feeling of gratification, enjoyment, or satisfaction. It's created by our senses. Pleasure is what happens when one or more of our senses stimulates the brain in a pleasant way. When you eat ice cream, the taste buds report to your brain that the ice cream is good, and you feel pleasure. When you are warm, dry, and comfortable in your bed at night, your senses report satisfaction to your brain on your physical state, and you feel pleasure. If you are camping in the snow, sleeping on the frozen ground, and your tent leaks, your senses report wet, cold, hard conditions. Your physical senses then report discomfort, and you won't feel pleasure.

Joy is the proactive choice to be grateful, glad, and happy, even when the senses aren't stimulating the brain in a pleasant way.

A mother giving birth has joy, even though she is in pain physically. Staying up late to bake someone special a birthday cake brings joy, even though it means less sleep and being tired the next day. Volunteering at the Church fundraiser all day Saturday can bring joy, even though you had to get up very early after a restless night to be there. Running a race can bring joy, even though your feet hurt, and you're tired. An act of service willingly done brings joy, even though we may sacrifice time, energy, or perhaps resources in order to serve others. Giving something we value highly to someone else brings joy, even though we immediately feel the loss of what we chose to give.

All of these examples are situations where we most often must choose to be joyful, in spite of the unpleasant sensations we experience. Even though, we aren't always conscious of making that choice. However, any of these situations could also be opportunities for someone to easily choose *not* to be joyful. How true are the words of the 14th Dalai Lama, *"Joy must arise from the level of your mind and not just your senses."*

Remembering all the terrible memories from my past does not bring me pleasure. Those memories are very painful. I would much rather never bring them to the surface again, much less write and talk about them regularly in front of people I have never met. However, helping someone else by sharing what I've learned because of what happened to me does bring me joy. It brings joy because I choose to be joyful about it.

Let me be clear about the difference between choosing joy in your heart and settling for *"less than"* in your life. We should always choose to be grateful for what we have, and we can always choose to have joy, regardless of how good or bad things may be. But, that doesn't mean we should quit striving to improve ourselves or our situation. Nor does it mean we should settle for unhappy circumstances because we aren't willing to make the necessary changes to improve our lives.

I meet far too many people who are unhappy. Yet, they are willing to settle for it because, miserable or not, they are comfortable with being unhappy. To stay the course, requires little or no additional effort. They would rather stay miserable in a known situation, environment, job, or relationship than risk trying something new that could potentially improve the rest of their life. If you aren't living an *"abundant life,"* it's time to change something.

However, don't forget to choose joy while you are implementing the necessary changes in your life.

PART III:
CROSSING FROM THERE TO HERE

CHAPTER TEN
CROSSING FROM REACTIVITY TO RESILIENCE

"What could have broken me made me."

~ Bob Chapman

Our behavior is determined by the choices we make. We have the incredible ability to choose how we respond to any given set of circumstances in life. Our behavior, thoughts, feelings, and emotions can be a conscious choice based on our values, rather than a product of our emotions and feelings.

When we are proactive as Stephen R. Covey defined it in his book, *The 7 Habits of Highly Effective People*, we respond to what happens to and around us based on the internal values we have carefully chosen. Our values determine the script we write for ourselves and our lives.

When we are reactive, we respond automatically based on our emotions and feelings. Failing to consciously choose our response to the situation, we therefore empower an external circumstance or even another person to control us.

Certainly, even very proactive people are influenced by what happens to them in life. But, their response to what happens is a careful, intentional, and value-based choice. We all have the gift of independent free will, also known as the freedom of choice. As a result, we all become the product of the choices we make.

This principle holds true universally. I recognized it somewhat unconsciously early on in my life. However, it was years later when I read *The 7 Habits of Highly Effective People* before I could articulate exactly what I had done to help myself survive the years of darkness, doubt, shame, and hopelessness I lived in from age 12 – 19.

By the time I was 19, I hated the life I was living. It was a life full of lies and deception. I felt I had three lives instead of one. The *public* Ria my family and friends thought I was, the *secret* Ria who learned to escape whenever she could by sneaking out of the house and meeting men from the internet, and the *shameful* Ria who had been groomed for nightly sexual activities with her father as he *"trained"* her to be a wife. His wife.

It didn't feel like life was worth living any longer. I had no hope that the future would be any better. I felt so completely trapped that I didn't think I would ever escape. How would I ever be able to leave? Even if I did leave, how would I support myself? I'd already tried to run away from home a couple of times. Each time, my father found me and took me back with him.

Once when I ran away, I made it as far as a hotel in Birmingham, Alabama. But with very little money, no job, and no options, I had no idea where I would go once the 11:00 am checkout time came the next morning. When my father tracked me down, I initially told him I wasn't going back with him. He left me alone to think about it. When he returned hours later, I felt I didn't have any other choice. He had spent many years manipulating me psychologically as he groomed me for his purposes. The emotional bondage he had over me had become incredibly strong. At that time, I believed returning home with him was better than starving alone on the streets.

I was depressed and felt completely hopeless. I sat in a chair in my bedroom one day and couldn't stop crying. If life wasn't going to get any better, why continue to live?

If you haven't been there, it's very difficult to imagine how desperately hopeless someone has to be to consider ending their life. I was a healthy 19 year old girl with many blessings, but I couldn't focus on the blessings because I was focused on the despair.

I was focused on a box of razor blades. I had heard or read somewhere that cutting your wrists and then bleeding to death in a tub of warm water would be nearly painless. It's very difficult today to think about how close I came to throwing away God's most precious gift to me – the gift of life.

In any situation in life, there are three steps to crossing the bridge from reactivity to resilience. They are self-awareness, imagination, and freedom of choice.

Self-awareness is the ability to step outside yourself and think about how you are feeling, what you are thinking, and the emotional state you are in. It's literally being aware of yourself. It's the ability to realize *"Hey, I'm feeling depressed (angry, upset, happy, frustrated, sad, mad). I'm thinking about* _____*."* Sitting in the chair in my bedroom that day, I had to become aware that I was feeling depressed and thinking about all the negative aspects of my situation.

Imagination is the ability to creatively think about different and better circumstances. It's the ability to create hope for yourself. Hope requires us to have a vision for the future. That vision must come from our imagination. I had to imagine the future COULD be better. Although, I didn't know how. I had to imagine it was still possible. I literally created a vision for the rest of my life that included freedom from my father's abuse.

Freedom of choice is simply the willpower to act on what we become aware of. It's choosing to imagine yourself living in a better future. It's a choice to focus on the positive instead of the negative. It's choosing to dance in the rain rather than mourning the sun.

Sitting in that chair, I had to choose to become aware and to imagine a better and hopeful future. Then, I had to choose to focus on that future. It's the ultimate freedom – the power to choose our response to what happens to us in life. That is the power of resilience.

CHAPTER ELEVEN
CROSSING FROM SHAME TO SELF-WORTH

"I am not what happened to me, I am what I choose to become."

~ Carl Jung

The most accurate and simplest definition I've heard of shame I learned from Brené Brown. She defines shame as *"I am a mistake"* versus guilt as *"I made a mistake."* That's an important distinction because until we truly understand what shame is, we can't overcome it.

When you feel like you are a mistake, you don't have any sense of self-worth. In other words, you feel like you are worse than a failure, you feel like you aren't good enough, like you are worthless and of no value to anyone or anything for any reason. A heavy burden of shame can crush someone completely and unfortunately, it's something we create within. As Eleanor Roosevelt said, *"No one can make you feel inferior without your consent."*

When we truly understand we can choose to be proactive to the external circumstances we are in, we realize no one can cause us to feel shame or to feel inferior. They may try to convince us of something, but whether we listen to them or not is something only we can control.

What happens all too often is someone says something or something happens that plants a tiny seed of doubt in your mind. That tiny seed has the potential to develop into a heavy ball and chain called shame. The thoughts we nurture are the thoughts we encourage to grow. If we nurture our positive thoughts, they will grow. If we nurture our negative thoughts, they will grow.

I was 12 years old in the early spring of 1993. My brother and mother took a trip. While they were gone, it snowed. My father and I were essentially snowed in for a day or so. Way back in the back of a forgotten drawer, my mother had a bunch of old lingerie. Since we were alone for a few days and he wasn't afraid of being interrupted, he made me put on each piece and *"model"* it for him. He was always commenting on how mature I looked, how grown up I was, and how much *"like a woman"* I already was.

Then, he made me lie down on the bed while he rubbed lotion on me, gradually getting closer to the areas I didn't feel comfortable having him touch. It wasn't the first time he had touched me like that, but this time he took it even further than before. I still had the white sheer negligee and panties on when he finally rubbed me between my legs. *"Oh,"* he panted, *"You're wet."*

With those three words, he had planted a seed in my mind that *I was a mistake.* After all, I knew what he was doing to me wasn't right. If my body was responding to it, then that must mean there was something wrong with me. He used it against me telling me I must like what he was doing since he could tell I was excited physically.

Since we were so isolated and homeschooled, I had been very sheltered growing up. I didn't know enough about sex to know what he meant, but I knew it was something sexual. I was instantly filled with revulsion for my body. I didn't want my body to respond to him.

I didn't know why it was happening. I hated his touch and the complete vulnerability I felt. I was already insecure and unsure about the changes I was experiencing growing up. My mother never told me what to expect as I transitioned from a girl into a woman. My father stripped away every bit of the physical privacy I needed as I discovered my body was beginning to change.

All I wanted was to wash and scrub all that revulsion I felt for my body off of me and then cover up as much of my body as possible. Instead, he made me sleep naked with him in his bed that night. The only thing I knew to do was to mentally shut out what was going on physically.

It was many years before I learned to love and appreciate my body instead of feeling either ashamed of it or as though it was the only thing that made me worth anything to anyone. To cross from shame to self-worth, there are two key steps.

REFUTE THE LIE

The first key step is to immediately refute any words, thoughts, or feelings that cause you to feel ashamed or inferior. I don't mean thoughts of guilt or *"I made a mistake"* but the words that make you feel you *are* a mistake.

If you don't like what you do, think about, say, or feel, then change it. Change what you value and the rest will follow suit. When you know you made a mistake, own it, work to correct it, and learn from it, so you don't repeat it.

CLAIM THE TRUTH

The second key step in overcoming shame is to claim the truth as your own. You are a child of God, and you are *"Fearfully and Wonderfully Made"* (Psalm 139:14) in His image. Regardless of the mistakes you have made, you are unique, precious to Him, and grace is available to you just waiting on you to claim it.

I know this seems too simple. The fact is, it is simple. It's a simple two-step process you can implement and repeat. That doesn't mean it's easy to do. But, it does get easier with practice. The more you do it, the quicker you will be able to block any thoughts of shame that dare enter the mind of God's perfectly imperfect creation.

CHAPTER TWELVE
CROSSING FROM GUILT TO GROWTH

"No one is a divine accident."

~ Desmond Tutu

Once we understand what shame is and how to overcome it, it's time to cross from guilt to growth. Remember the difference: shame is *"I am a mistake"* while guilt is *"I made a mistake."*

We all make mistakes. That's a fact. It isn't a good thing or a bad thing, it's simply the way it is. Growth comes when we learn from the mistakes we have made.

Mistakes create opportunities for learning. One of the human learning models is learning what doesn't work as we attempt to learn what does work. Think about a baby learning to walk. She tries, fails, and tries again. She repeats the process over and over until she *learns* what does work by first learning what doesn't work.

Mistakes are often how we *"learn things the hard way."* I made plenty of mistakes while learning to cook. More than once, I ended up with overcooked food before I learned to pay close attention to the stove.

Most often, we make our biggest mistakes when we're interacting with people. Sometimes, we learn who is not trustworthy by extending trust to the wrong person and then being hurt by them. Or, we may hurt someone else intentionally or unintentionally and pay the price of losing their trust. A careless comment or thoughtless remark meant to be a joke can often hurt someone. If we aren't careful, those types of mistakes may destroy relationships.

Unfortunately, we don't always learn from our mistakes. Not learning is bad enough, but often we experience something much worse than not learning from the mistake. We end up losing confidence in ourselves because we made the mistake. We let the guilt from the mistakes we made in the past continue to drag us down, thus negatively affecting our future. My friend Tonya Spence said, *"Don't let the circumstances of the past dim the brilliance of your future."*

When I left home at 19, I chose not to go to the authorities and press charges against my father. I was struggling with the shame of my past, and I didn't want to discuss it publicly.

Right or wrong, that was the choice I made. I have lived with that choice for the past 17 years and now acknowledge it may very well have been a mistake.

Maybe, it wasn't a mistake for me? Maybe, it was? Who knows? I may have healed sooner if, instead of walling up my past back then, I had talked about it.

Regardless of how it affected me, it almost certainly was a mistake that had consequences for my brother and mother. Yes, it would have been awful to go through the investigation and legal process in 2000. But, they would have had the opportunity to be free from my father's influence and the oppression he has over them.

We can choose our actions, but not the consequences that flow from those actions. My choice in 2000 was to protect myself. I felt that was the best choice for me. However, the consequences of my choice affected many other people besides me. This is why it's so easy to feel guilt when we believe we made a mistake.

Compared to the mistakes we make that hurt others, those that only hurt us are much easier to get over.

However, growth can come from guilt. Crossing from guilt to growth is a process that can be broken down into three steps: Respond, Repair, and Reflect.

RESPOND

Respond immediately when you realize you have made

a mistake. Take ownership of your mistake and acknowledge it. Sometimes, this can be done privately between you and the other person. Sometimes, it should be done very publicly. Authentically acknowledging and accepting responsibility for your mistakes will go a long way toward increasing your influence with everyone who is watching. No one expects you to be perfect, but they do expect you to know and admit when you aren't.

REPAIR

Repair what you can. This may mean making a sincere apology and trying to make amends. Trust is a delicate thing. When you make a mistake with people, you may damage or outright destroy the trust in the relationship. It will take time to earn it back. The other person will decide how much trust you regain and when it will happen. The relationship may never be the same, but you can and should try to repair it.

REFLECT

Reflect on what you did wrong and what you could have done differently. In order for us to learn from our mistakes and not repeat them, we must take the time to intentionally shift our perspective and see the situation from another side. This takes time and a very honest look at yourself, your values, words, thoughts, and actions. Intentionally reflect. Then, forgive yourself and move on. But, don't miss the opportunity to learn what not to do next time. As Nelson Boswell said, *"The difference between greatness and mediocrity is often how an individual views mistakes."*

CHAPTER THIRTEEN
CROSSING FROM HURT TO HAPPINESS

"The state of your life is nothing more than a reflection of the state of your mind."

~ Wayne Dyer

There isn't a hierarchy on suffering. What you are going through, or have gone through, may seem much worse than what I experienced growing up, or perhaps it may seem less *"significant."* Regardless of how what you're going through looks like to outsiders, when you are going through adversity it can drag you down.

At some point, we try to find a coping mechanism or a survival strategy. My survival mechanism was to spend as much energy and time as possible pretending what was happening with my father wasn't really happening. As long as I could ignore it all, I thought it couldn't hurt me mentally. However, that's not a survival strategy I recommend. It didn't serve me well. Rather than deal with my emotions, I simply pretended they didn't exist.

I was hurting inside in so many ways. The abuse started to affect my daily life. I was almost 18 when I stopped really caring about myself. I would *"forget"* to wash my hair for several days at a time, allowing it to get oily and greasy. It didn't really seem to matter to me. I didn't see the point of making the extra effort.

I was feeling self-conscious about my body, but my father always wanted me to wear clothes that were too tight, too short, or too revealing. I felt strange around other girls my age. I didn't shave my legs, wear makeup, or talk about jobs, boyfriends, or whatever *"normal"* 18 year old girls talk about. I didn't have much in common with anyone. No one was living the life I was living.

We didn't have a healthy lifestyle when I was growing up. My parents didn't focus on health and wellness. My friends' families were all very health conscious, eating organic whole foods and limiting junk food. My family would show up to the homeschool picnic with a box of donuts. My parents were also overweight. To me, exercise was something for those who were fat and wanted to lose weight. I wasn't fat, so I didn't exercise. And, it didn't seem like a big deal when I started having an extra *"treat."*

I thought to myself *"I deserve a treat."* as I carried a few extra cookies to my bedroom. They were good and made me feel good. They couldn't be bad for me, or so I thought. I had no idea sugar was bad for me, or that it was so addicting. I only knew I wanted something to make me feel good. It wasn't long before I progressed to entire boxes of brown sugar and leftover cartons of cake frosting. I would eat it with a spoon until I was sick and occasionally threw it all back up.

I had always been thin, but not surprisingly, I started gaining weight. When my father realized it, he took me to the local gym and paid for my membership, so I could start exercising. He allowed me to go there only because there was a special room upstairs where women could work out, and no men were permitted.

It was one of the best things that happened to me. When I started exercising, a lightbulb came on in my mind. I noticed I felt stronger, more confident, and more empowered when I was exercising. I liked those feelings much more than when I made myself sick eating sweets. I developed a new habit that served me much better.

I quit overeating, reduced my sugar intake, and started taking better care of myself. My father also started letting me wear some makeup and nail polish, but only as long as I wasn't going anywhere where there might be boys.

Often, when we are hurting, we try to numb the pain with something that makes us feel good. We create a coping mechanism or a survival strategy for self-defense.

When we repeat the behavior over and over, it becomes a habit. Sometimes, those habits can damage us as quickly as whatever we are trying to escape from.

BUILD GOOD HABITS

To cross from hurt to happiness, make sure your habits and behaviors are serving you well. This requires taking a good hard look at your life and lifestyle, and may be uncomfortable. When you can honestly say, *"This isn't serving me or taking me where I want to go"* and decrease it, eliminate it, or limit it, you will be far better off.

You can overindulge in anything: exercise, food, alcohol, drugs, sugar, shopping, sex, games, gambling, social media, TV, etc. The list is endless. It's not necessarily the action itself, it's why we are doing it that can be destructive. When the habit controls you instead of you controlling it, there is a problem.

It's important to find the right balance. If you enjoy eating chocolate, then eat some chocolate. Just don't eat too much of it, and don't eat it every day. I still enjoy sweet things, but I keep the portion size healthy.

If you discover you have created a habit doing something that isn't serving you well, it's easier to overcome it by doing something positive in its place. For example, if you drink too much soda, try cutting back initially and add in something healthier. Later on, you may choose to eliminate it all together.

Resilient people realize they can build good habits to help them be happy, rather than bad habits that will only compound and increase the hurt. As Ralph Waldo Emerson said, *"Don't be pushed by your problems. Be led by your dreams."*

CHAPTER FOURTEEN
CROSSING FROM FURY TO FORGIVENESS

"Forgiveness does not change the past, but it does enlarge the future."

~ Paul Boese

If there was a hierarchy of most *"Christ-like"* words, *"forgive"* would have to be at the top of my list.

"Forgive" is a verb. It's an action that begins inside our hearts and then extends outward to others. We don't feel forgiveness and then act on it. We act on it and then feel it. Forgiving is one of the simplest things to do. Yet ironically for most of us, it's difficult.

Nearly everyone has someone they don't want to forgive. A business partner who cheated you, a salesman who was less than honest, a co-worker who threw you under the bus to look better for the boss, a spouse who hurt you, or a friend who betrayed you.

What so many of us fail to realize about forgiveness is we don't have any right to refuse forgiveness for a wrong done us. Jesus died to forgive our sins. He died to forgive my sins. He died to forgive your sins. He also died to forgive the sins of the person who wronged you. Jesus has already paid our debts in full. We do not have any right to claim it.

C. S. Lewis had this to say about forgiveness, *"This is what Jesus did. He told people that their sins were forgiven, and never waited to consult all the other people whom their sins had undoubtedly injured."*

In other words, Jesus forgave all sins. Once a debt is paid, another cannot claim it.

Regardless of who it was and how they wronged you, the fury, anger, and violence you may have is not yours to hold on to. Jesus died to pay back the debt they owed you and the wrong they did to you.

However, let me be very clear. Even with forgiveness,

there may still be consequences.

As I mentioned previously, more than 17 years ago when I last talked to my father, it was made clear if he left me and my family alone I wouldn't press charges for the seven years of sexual abuse, rape, physical abuse, and instances where he allowed other men to abuse me too.

Honestly and selfishly, I didn't really want to go to the authorities and press charges in 2000 because I didn't think I could handle the questions, the pressure, and the shame of the world knowing what my father had done to me. I didn't and still don't hold any bitterness or anger. I didn't believe battling things out through the legal system would benefit anyone. So, I chose to move forward.

My parents moved out of state and cut off all contact with everyone else in the family. They returned unopened birthday cards from my grandparents and didn't attend the recent funeral of my grandfather, my mother's father.

However, my father recently inserted himself back into the picture. Essentially, he started harassing my grandparents (his parents) in 2016 through letters and was pressuring them to *"Pretend Ria doesn't exist, so you can have a relationship with me."* It started as *"Let's get together,"* but his letters turned hateful very quickly. He didn't keep his end of the deal I made in 2000. Although I had forgiven him, it's clear he no longer believes there will be consequences for his actions from all those years ago.

However, I know something he doesn't. The woman I am today isn't the same scared and ashamed 19-year-old girl he knew back then. The woman I am today won't be bullied into silence. I have already forgiven him for the wrongs he did to me – and if he had not decided to come back into my life and my family's life, I would never have pressed charges in 2016. But, the consequence of his choice to re-enter my life will be a trial where he must confront his past actions publicly.

As Rick Warren said, *"Forgiveness is letting go of the past. Trust has to do with future behavior."* Forgiving and trusting are two completely different things. I have forgiven my father for the past, but I don't trust his future behavior. He has never made an attempt to earn back my trust.

Forgiveness doesn't mean you let someone bully you afterward. Forgiveness does mean the state of your heart is not bitter, angry, or resentful. Forgiveness is about *you*, not others. Others may not even know you have forgiven them. Others knowing isn't important. You don't forgive for others. You forgive for yourself.

Forgiveness is the choice to exercise your independent will and refuse to become reactive based on your emotions. To cross from fury to forgiveness, there are two critical steps.

The first step is to acknowledge the hurt. Acknowledge the pain. Acknowledge the wrongs done.

And then, choose to let it go. If it helps, write it down on a piece of paper. Then, literally shred it into pieces. Or, burn it. Or, bury it. Whatever it takes, even if you must physically act out releasing it from your hand, choose to let it go. Say out loud, *"Jesus died to forgive that person's sins, including this one. The debt has already been paid."*

Within 24 hours of learning my father had re-entered my life in 2016, I contacted the authorities, scheduled an appointment, and then walked into the sheriff's office. I held my head high and filed an 11 page report with many details describing what he did to me. The statute of limitations has run out on many of his offenses, including incest, but not on all offenses. There will always be consequences for our actions. His choice to return was also a choice to face a trial. I have already acknowledged the hurt, and I have already released it.

CHAPTER FIFTEEN
CROSSING FROM FOG TO FOCUS

"A conviction that you are a child of God gives you a feeling of comfort in your self-worth. It means that you can find strength in the balm of Christ. It will help you meet the heartaches and challenges with faith and serenity."

~ James E. Faust

If you've been driving a car for more than a few months, odds are you have experienced a time when you had to drive through fog. When a thick, heavy fog blankets the road around you, the scenery around you fades away, the road itself can become difficult to see, and it becomes almost impossible to see potential hazards or even other cars.

There are times when we also experience *"fog"* in our lives. It's most common during times of change, transition, and uncertainty. It's easy to become disoriented or feel lost in the *"fog"* when life is changing drastically, and it can be downright scary.

Focus provides clarity. When we focus, we clearly see what we're working toward, driving to, and striving for. The more focused we are and the more intentional we are, the greater our chances of success are.

While navigating through *"fog,"* it's difficult to remain focused. When we lose focus, we are likely to find ourselves drifting off course. When that happens, the odds of us reaching our destination are diminished.

After I left my parents' home, there were several weeks of *"fog."* My entire world had turned upside down during this life changing transition. I was navigating new relationships, new freedom, new possibilities, a new gym, and even a new city. I wasn't sure where I was going or how I was going to get there, but I wanted to figure it out quickly.

The future looked uncertain, and uncertainty was

scary, especially for a 19 year old girl who had just experienced seven years of physical, sexual, and emotional abuse. As bad as my situation had been, it had become familiar. I didn't like the new *"fog"* of uncertainty.

There has been plenty of *"fog"* since then, and I've had many opportunities to sharpen my skills while navigating through it. I've learned there are three important steps to take when crossing from *"fog"* to focus.

CHOOSE FAITH OVER FEAR

You cannot have fear if you have faith. As Terry A. Smith said, *"Fear is faith moving in the wrong direction."* When you're trying to move beyond the *"fog,"* make a conscious choice to choose faith instead of fear. Yes, the future may be uncertain. But when you choose faith, you replace the fear. With faith, you will no longer fear the *"fog."*

Rich Sterns, CEO of World Vision stated it this way, *"Whatever we are facing, we can rest in the assurance that the outcome does not depend on our strength, but on God's."*

It's much easier to choose faith over fear when you remember God has a plan for you. It doesn't matter if you can't see it or don't know what it is because there's always a plan. When we choose faith, we simply trust in His plan and provision. Fear will fade away.

NARROW YOUR FOCUS

When you're feeling overwhelmed by the *"fog,"* pause. Determine the most important step you should take. Don't worry about the next 10 steps or the next 100 steps. Simply identify the next step and focus on taking it. Once you have taken the step, repeat the process.

When I left my parents' home, my *"next step"* was to find a job. So, I didn't think about college or getting a GED. I focused on the next step: getting a job. I went to the state career center, took a typing test, and put in some applications. The process takes time, so I left there without having found a job. I bought a newspaper and looked at the classifieds, but there weren't any jobs I was qualified for. Next, I started driving around and discovered a few places with *"We're Hiring"* signs posted. I walked into one of them. When I walked out, I had a job. Then, and only then, was it time for me to begin focusing on the next step.

TAKE TIME TO REST

When we are crossing from *"fog"* to focus, it's important to remember to take time for rest and renewal. You may be feeling stressed and anxiety may creep in leaving you feeling as if you don't have time to stop and rest. However, resting may be the best thing to do.

You aren't losing any momentum if you take time to rest while you're stuck in the *"fog."* Sometimes, the rest and renewal is exactly what's needed to bring focus and clarity back.

When I'm feeling overwhelmed in the *"fog,"* I make sure to take time out for myself. The thicker the *"fog"* I'm going through, the more intentional I become about taking time to rest. There may be 100 things on my *"to do"* list, but I still make sure I take time for renewal and exercise. Sometimes, simply slowing down in the *"fog"* brings everything back into focus.

CHAPTER SIXTEEN
CROSSING FROM ANXIETY TO ACCEPTANCE

"If you carry joy in your heart, you can heal any moment."

~ Carlos Santana

Experiencing anxiety is something nearly everyone has suffered from at times. A trigger occurs and you experience anxious feelings and perhaps physical symptoms as well.

Please note: This chapter is not intended to replace appropriate therapy or treatment. What I want to address in this chapter is the general, *"normal"* anxiety that can affect our daily lives. **If you experience severe anxiety, panic attacks, or mental disturbances, please seek out treatment by a qualified doctor or therapist.**

There is no doubt suffering from sexual abuse and the shame I felt affected me in many ways, but perhaps the worst was the effect on my sexual relationship with my husband.

I had never experienced a sexual relationship where sex was an expression of intimacy and love. When Mack asked me if I was being sexually abused by my father in 2000, I acknowledged it and felt terrible fear. I was afraid he would no longer want me because I felt dirty, used, and expected to be discarded. Instead, Mack has always made an incredible effort to make me feel loved, valued, appreciated, and special as a person and as his wife.

I still experience anxiety in many ways. If I turn the corner in the grocery store and unexpectedly see a man who resembles my father, I feel like someone punched me in the stomach. While trying a new shampoo once, I poured it onto my hair in the shower. As I was massaging it into my scalp, the smell hit me. I became physically sick because I knew instantly it was the same shampoo my father had used. I immediately threw it away.

I still have flashbacks, terrible nightmares, and there

are some things I won't do because doing them would bring back bad memories or feelings. My anxiety hasn't disappeared magically. I have simply learned to cross from anxiety to acceptance. That doesn't mean my problems have gone away. It does mean I have learned how to move beyond them.

I don't pretend to have all the answers or that this is a *"one size fits all"* answer to your problems. Please talk to a doctor if you feel you need help.

However, I do want to share some techniques that have helped me cross from anxiety to acceptance.

ACKNOWLEDGE THE PROBLEM

Nothing ever gets better because you pretend it isn't a problem. Denial of the issue won't resolve it, no matter how much you want it to. Start by acknowledging the problem and admitting how it affects you. If you have anxiety around sex because of a history of abuse, then talk with your partner about it openly and honestly. It may take time to work through the issue, but you will be working through it together.

If you have flashbacks and PTSD because of the experiences you had in the military, share with your loved ones how certain triggers affect you. Ask for their support in minimizing those triggers until you learn to manage the effects. Talk to a therapist who specializes in helping veterans overcome PTSD. If that's too much, find a best friend who will listen completely without judgment and love you anyway. At our core, we all want to know we are loved. If you can't find a best friend, talk to God. He will ALWAYS listen without judgment and love you anyway.

FOCUS ON POSITIVE THOUGHTS

When we are experiencing anxiety, our focus is on all the negatives in the situation. Anxiety is often worry and fear related to what we cannot control. We don't like feeling out of control, and this creates anxiety.

When that happens, refocus your thoughts on something positive. Bring your energy and focus back to something you can control. If you are feeling anxious in the grocery store because something triggered a painful memory, stop, take a deep breath, and remind yourself you are a free adult. If you want to leave the grocery store, you can. Try thinking through in advance what I call the *"What if, then what?"* scenario, as in *"What if (insert anxiety causing situation), then what I will do is (insert best case scenario resolution)."*

BE YOUR BEST SELF

It's important for everyone to know what their *"best self"* looks like. Your *"best self"* is the version of you who is the best expression of your true self on your best day. My *"best self"* is very intentional about all the dimensions of my life but especially about taking care of my physical fitness. Perhaps because I didn't value my health for a long time, I now maintain a very healthy lifestyle. I don't always get it right, but I know what my *"best self"* looks like. When I'm anxious, I try to consider what my *"best self"* would do in the situation – and then I do it. As Eleanor Roosevelt said, *"You gain strength, courage, and confidence by every experience in which you really stop to look fear in the face. You are able to say to yourself, 'I lived through this horror. I can take the next thing that comes along.'"*

CHAPTER SEVENTEEN
CROSSING FROM HATE TO HEALING

"An eye for an eye only ends up making the whole world blind."
~ Mahatma Gandhi

Dicitionary.com defines hate as, *"dislike intensely, or passionately; feel extreme aversion for or hostility toward"* something or someone. For the sake of this chapter, we'll focus on hate toward someone. It's important to distinguish between the bitterness, resentment, anger, and fury toward someone *because they have wronged you* and the hate you feel toward someone *because of something inside you.*

For example, it's not usual in sports to hear someone say they *"hate"* the team's rival. That's not because they have been personally wronged by the rival. It's because they have created negative emotions inside themselves toward their rival. Perhaps, appropriately channeled, the emotions can inspire improved athletic performance as the team battles the rival.

When hate becomes an all-consuming emotion creating negative energy in all aspects of our lives, it will only cause us problems. That type of hate is an emotion we create because we feel the lack of something inside ourselves.

Hate is an emotion we direct toward others because of something *we* feel, and isn't caused by others at all. Fury is an emotion we direct toward others because of something *they* did or said.

Hate directed toward others conveys far more about the person hating than the person being hated. As the Dalai Lama said, *"We can never obtain peace in the outer world until we make peace with ourselves."*

The opposite of hate is love. We create hate when we don't love enough. Hate will never bring about healing, only love can do that. The key is realizing that instead of hating someone less, we need to love ourselves and others more. Healing takes place when this happens.

I was about 14 years old when my father decided to put a pool in our yard. Our entire family got excited about the project, planning the layout of the deck, and looking forward to the fun we expected it to bring. Not only would it be a relief in the hot summer months, but it would also be something I could invite my friends over to enjoy. Since my father limited my opportunities to leave and spend time elsewhere with friends, I was always looking for ways to get them to my house.

We put in an above ground pool. During the two weeks it took to fill it up (we were on well water, and the supply was limited), our family took a trip to Walmart to buy groceries and whatever else we needed.

I was getting a bathing suit this trip. My father had decided it should be a bikini. My mother was with us, but she didn't say anything as he helped me select a few to try on. I went into the dressing room to change, but he told me to come out and *"model"* for them, which meant him since he had to approve which one I would get.

I didn't want to come out of the dressing room. I felt very self-conscious about my body, and I had never had a two-piece bathing suit. I peeked out of the dressing room and waited until only my parents were around before I took a few steps out.

My mother started snickering right away. *"She's got saddlebags!"* she said as she laughed out loud.

"Saddlebags" were the leather bags I put around my horse's saddle to carry things in. What on earth did she mean? I had no idea. But, I knew *"saddlebags"* must have meant something awful, and I didn't want them.

My father later explained what she meant. The term apparently meant someone who has fat on the outer thigh area. I was mortified. I felt very vulnerable and insecure about my body already because of what he had been doing to me.

Now, I had something else and someone else to focus on. I started to resent my mother for making fun of me. I developed hostility toward her. But, it was all rooted in the fact that I didn't have confidence in myself. My security and self-confidence was based on being physically attractive because that's what I was learning from father. His grooming had taught me that being physically attractive and *"pretty"* meant I was *"good."* So to me, her words implied I wasn't *"pretty"* and therefore I wasn't *"good."*

I spent several weeks that summer resenting my mother and that bathing suit every time I had to put it on. It wasn't until I was able to get another one that I let my resentment towards her go. I finally realized what I looked like wasn't her fault and how I felt about what I looked like wasn't her fault either. I also realized I still loved her in spite of it all.

To cross from hate to healing, we must realize the lack inside ourselves that causes the insecurity we are feeling. We must be able to cultivate empathy instead. Empathy will allow us to see things from the perspective of others. Daniel Pink said, *"Empathy is about standing in someone else's shoes, feeling with his or her heart, seeing with his or her eyes."*

If my mother had practiced empathy outside that dressing room, she would have probably been more considerate. I was able to practice empathy and understood it was simply a thoughtless remark, not hate towards me. I also realized words only have meaning when we attach significance to them. Mahatma Ghandi said, *"Nobody can hurt me without my permission."*

CHAPTER EIGHTEEN
CROSSING FROM FEAR TO FREEDOM

"The graveyard is the richest place on earth, because it is here that you will find all the hopes and dreams that were never fulfilled, the books that were never written, the songs that were never sung, the inventions that were never shared, the cures that were never discovered, all because someone was too afraid to take that first step."

~ Les Brown

Everyone faces fear. The question is, *"What will we do when we face fear?"* Nelson Mandela said *"I learned that courage was not the absence of fear, but the triumph over it. The brave man is not he who does not feel afraid, but he who conquers that fear."*

Fear is the emotion we create when we worry. We create fear by telling ourselves all the bad things that could happen. What we focus on expands. To overcome fear, we must identify a reason to move forward that is stronger than our fear. Overcoming fear means allowing our core values to guide us, rather than allowing the emotions of worry, concern, or fear to control us.

The vast majority of our fears are completely unfounded anyway. In his book *The Worry Cure,* Robert Leahy cites a statistic stating 85% of what we are afraid of never happens.

Fear is something created by our thoughts. In the words of Dale Carnegie, *"Fear doesn't exist anywhere except in your mind."* That's why different people have different fears – because they think different thoughts.

Fear is one of the most basic emotions and can be healthy when warranted. But far too often, fear holds us back and prevents us from moving forward.

Fear has impacted me on many occasions, but it prevented me from moving forward several years ago when I was working in a doctor's office. It was a good place to work with regular hours. I liked the work, and the doctor I was working for was nice. But, after being there nearly a year, I had learned most of what I could learn related to my role, and the future at that office was pretty limited. I knew it was time to move on and find another job, so I could keep growing and learning.

But, I was afraid to leave and try something new. What if I didn't like the new office as well? What if I didn't like my new co-workers? What if they didn't like me?

That was perhaps my biggest fear – the fear of meeting new people and building new relationships. It had been several years since I had left my parents' abusive home, but my social skills still weren't too good. I was always stressed out in new social situations. I was sure I would say or do the wrong things. Most often, I just stayed quiet. I was afraid people wouldn't like me. Or, that I wouldn't like them.

My fears caused me to stay several more months before I was able to work up the courage to apply for other jobs. My fear of the unknown, relative to meeting new people, was holding me back. But, I didn't know what to do about it. Several years passed before I learned that regardless of my lack of ability to connect and communicate with people, I could develop and improve those skills intentionally. I shared much of what I learned about connecting and communicating with others in my book, *Straight Talk: The Power of Effective Communication.*

That was the last time I let fear control me, but it's certainly not the last time I felt fear. We all have fears and will find ourselves afraid at some point for some reason. The key is to learn how to control your fear instead of letting your fear control you.

There are three steps that will help you cross from fear to freedom.

IDENTIFY YOUR FEAR

When you find yourself not taking action or not moving forward, take the time to really think about why. You may be afraid of many things. Fear of failure. Fear of making a mistake. Fear of not being popular. Fear that others may not agree with your decision. Stephen R. Covey referred to the *"Circle of Concern,"* where everything you can't control or influence is located. If you venture into the *"Circle of Concern,"* you are simply wasting valuable time and energy because you have no control and no influence.

IDENTIFY WHAT YOU CAN CONTROL

Once you have identified your fear, stop focusing on it. Instead, make a list of everything you can control, influence, or cause to happen. This is where very successful people invest their time and energy – on the things they *can* do. If you focus your time, energy, and effort on the things you can control, you will find fewer things remain in your *"Circle of Concern."*

TAKE ACTION

If the situation is out of your control, there isn't any reason to worry about it. Worrying won't help. Not moving forward at all or never taking a risk isn't an option for very successful leaders. They see mistakes as learning opportunities, failures as strength builders, and the unknown as a potential place for positive things to happen. As Muhammad Ali said, *"He who is not courageous enough to take risks will accomplish nothing in life."*

CHAPTER NINETEEN
CROSSING FROM PAIN TO PURPOSE

"Let your name be remembered for the good you have done, the joy you have spread and the love you have shared."

~ Mother Teresa

Life is filled with pain.

A mother loses her child to a drowning accident. A husband loses his wife to breast cancer. A daughter loses her innocence to sexual abuse. A family loses each other when loved ones are torn apart by blame.

I don't have to tell you life hurts sometimes. Your story may not be the same as my story. But, I know you have a story, and somewhere in your story is a chapter on pain. And, there's likely more than one chapter.

When we are going through something painful, the biggest question is *"Why?"* As in, *"Why me? Why now? Why not somebody else? Why did I have to go through this? Why did she get sick? Why did he have to die? Why did my father abuse me?"*

We may never know the answers, but we can rest assured there are answers. There is a purpose to our pain even when we don't know why. Sometimes, we know why immediately. Sometimes, it may take years as it did in my case before I could see the purpose behind my pain.

God doesn't cause the pain in our lives. But, He can use it. And, when we allow Him to use it, we cross from pain to purpose. As Rick Warren, author of *The Purpose Driven Life* said, *"Your most effective ministry will come out of your deepest hurts."*

LET GO OF THE PAIN AND THE PAST

We will all face struggles and challenges. Overcoming those challenges is what will make us stronger and better prepared for a bigger challenge down the road. But, we must be willing to let go of the pain from the past.

John C. Maxwell had this to say about the past, *"The past is gone and outside your control. You are responsible for not allowing it to control you in the present."*

Let it go. Put it behind you, and move on. We cannot change the past. We can only learn from it.

The past has passed. While you need to remember the past and learn from it, it's important to move beyond it. Don't let old, emotional baggage weigh you down or clutter your life today.

Sometimes, we must let go of what's behind us before we can reach what's in front of us.

Steve Maraboli said, *"How many of us walk around being weighed down by the baggage of our journey? You can't possibly embrace that new relationship, that new companion, that new career, that new friendship, or that new life you want while you're still holding on to the baggage of the last one. Let go...and allow yourself to embrace what is waiting for you right at your feet."*

EMBRACE THE PURPOSE

You are created, called, and destined for a purpose. God created you for a purpose and called you to that purpose in this exact time. God wants you to live more fully into your purpose because it fulfills what He wants for you.

As William James said, *"The best use of life is to spend it for something that outlasts it."*

Discovering and growing into our purpose is a process we should joyfully seek out intentionally. It's very rare to discover our purpose completely by accident, so we must live intentionally in order to grow spiritually and personally into the shoes God created for us to wear. And then, we will be walking in His footsteps.

You are unique. You are special. You are precious.

There is no one else who has been given exactly the same personality, talents, abilities, and experiences that God equipped you with. He first equips you. And then, He empowers you.

We often feel like we aren't *"enough,"* aren't good enough, aren't strong enough, or aren't worth enough. Sometimes, we feel like we aren't equipped to carry out God's plan for us because it is so much bigger than we are.

You are enough. You are enough to carry out the tasks God gives you because if you weren't ready, He wouldn't have called you. He already knows it. You need to know it.

If your life feels empty at this moment, that's a sign you have yet to come completely into God's plan for you.

If you feel like you haven't yet found your calling or God's purpose for your life, it's important to understand that doesn't make you inadequate or less precious in the eyes of Jesus. Resist the urge to compare yourself to someone else and to think you aren't as good as they are.

When we compare ourselves to others, we are failing to live our unique identity and purpose. We weren't created to be anyone else and shouldn't strive to be someone else. We should only strive to be our best self.

God challenges us to accept the responsibility for our life, but He does not challenge us beyond what we can handle. You are enough. Accept the responsibility, acknowledge it won't be easy and you won't always get it right, and be willing to learn from your mistakes.

God created you, called you, and He crafted you with special talents, gifts, and strengths, so you can fulfill His plan for you. Your life is a book filled with blank pages. You will fill the pages each day one choice at a time.

CHAPTER TWENTY
CROSSING FROM BROKEN TO BEAUTIFUL

"The world breaks everyone, and afterward, some are strong at the broken places."

~ Ernest Hemingway

We've all been broken. But, we can learn to heal. We can cross over from broken to beautiful.

Beautiful in spite of the brokenness?

No. Beautiful *because* of the brokenness.

Many people reach out to me with a story of hardship, grief, or loss in their own lives or the life of someone they love. I feel their pain. Yet, I know that what happened to us isn't most important. What's most important is who we become because of what happened.

We all have a story to tell. We've all experienced things in life that have shaped us, molded us, defined us, and refined us. Look at those who have overcome incredible adversity: Les Brown, Liz Murray, Bethany Hamilton, and so many others. These are examples of people who didn't allow their stories to define them, but rather allowed their stories to refine them. Define or refine, what's the difference?

When you allow your story and painful experiences to define the rest of your life, you become broken by your story.

When you overcome your story and painful experiences by allowing them to refine you, you become better because of your story. You are a warrior. You are strong. You are special. You are beautiful in *spirit*.

How we frame our story or experience determines whether it will define who we are or whether it will refine who we become.

If you can frame your story, you can reframe your story. It's your story to tell. How you frame your story as you tell your story is up to you.

Reframing allows you to choose to become a survivor instead of remaining a victim. Reframing our stories helps us realize we aren't victims at all. Reframing allows us to become strong, resilient people refined by our experiences, but not defined by them.

It's not the facts of our life that determine our hope for the future. It's what we tell ourselves about those facts. Some people with painful stories see themselves as victims and feel God has abandoned them. Other people choose to be victors rising above what happened to them and feel God is alongside them.

As Maya Angelou said, *"I can be changed by what happens to me…"* And, no doubt I was changed. There is a part of me that wants to mourn the girl I could have been growing up. There is part of me that wants to point fingers and blame my father for taking me upstairs and taking my clothes off when I was 12 years old and home alone with him. There is a part of me that wishes I had not grown up thinking the definition of parental love included sexual attraction and sexual gratification.

But, it's the second half of Maya Angelou's quote that makes it so powerful, *"…but I refuse to be reduced by it."*

That's the difference between a victim and a victor. Yes, we are changed by what happens to us in life. But, we decide how. We decide if we will or won't be reduced by what happens to us.

You see, there is a big difference between *"I didn't die,"* and *"I learned to live again."* **The difference is the choice to see adversity as a growth experience and an opportunity to become stronger instead of choosing to see it as a storm that crushes us.**

Changed by what happened to me, I spent several years in the mindset of *"I didn't die."* But four years ago, I made the choice to refuse to be reduced by it, and *"I learned to live again."* I will not be reduced by what happened to me.

That my friends is true freedom. It's the number one key for becoming resilient. When you realize the past or present can only hurt you if you allow it to, you can choose not to allow it to hurt you. And then, you find peace, happiness, joy, and abundance are within your reach. Unfortunately, some people will spend a lifetime searching for what they already have the ability to possess.

Psalm 139 reveals the complete knowledge God has of us. The Psalm reassures us that God knows us, understands us, leads us, and comforts us. He created each and every detail of *you*. Indeed, when we consider the miracle of the human body from conception and birth through life and death, we realize we are all *"fearfully and wonderfully made."*

We are already beautiful in the eyes of God.

You are beautiful. You are unique. You are cherished. You are loved. You are *"Fearfully and Wonderfully Made."*

Choosing to let go and embrace the joy in life, regardless of what we are going through, or have gone through, is a choice each of us can make. But, each of us must make it for ourselves. No one can do it for us. There aren't any shortcuts, secrets, or instant cures. It's simply getting up one day at a time and choosing to be grateful. I get up every day and decide to be better because of my past, instead of being bitter about it.

So can you.

ACKNOWLEDGMENTS

I am grateful to be able to share God's glory by telling my story. God doesn't cause the pain in our lives but, He can use it. He has used the pain of my experiences to bring hope and freedom to many people around the world.

There are so many people who have supported me over the years I can't possibly count them all. People come into our lives. We either help them, or they help us. Both opportunities are a blessing, and I'm grateful for them all.

I'm grateful to my husband, Mack, for the feedback, synergy, ideas, proof-reading, editing, support, and for being my biggest cheerleader. But most of all, I'm grateful to you for loving the scared, bruised, battered, bound, and broken 19 year old girl I was, and for your love and continued patience with the perfectly imperfect, still a work in progress, woman you have helped me become.

ABOUT THE AUTHOR

Like many, Ria faced adversity in life. Raised on an isolated farm in Alabama, she was sexually abused by her father from age 12 – 19. Desperate to escape, she left home at 19 without a job, a car, or even a high school diploma. Ria learned to be resilient, not only surviving, but thriving. She worked her way through college, earning her MBA with a cumulative 4.0 GPA, and had a successful career in the corporate world of administrative healthcare.

Ria's background includes more than 10 years in administrative healthcare with several years in management including Director of Compliance and Regulatory Affairs for a large healthcare organization. Ria's responsibilities included oversight of thousands of organizational policies, organizational compliance with all State and Federal regulations, and responsibility for several million dollars in Medicare appeals.

Ria has a passion for health and wellness and is a certified group fitness instructor. She has completed several marathons and half-marathons and won both the Alabama and Georgia Women's State Mountain Biking Championships in 2011 and 2012.

Today, Ria is a motivational leadership speaker and author of 10 books. Ria and her husband, Mack Story, co-founded Top Story Leadership which offers motivational speaking, leadership training, coaching, and consulting. Watch Ria's TEDx talk, *Bridges Out of the Past* online at: RiaStory.com/TEDX

Excerpt from *Beyond Bound and Broken*, by Ria Story

Forgiving God

Where was God when I was suffering? Where was God when my dad told me his only regret was *"not starting sooner"* so he could have watched my breasts develop? Where was God when I hated my dad for taking away my privacy? Where was God when I found myself so ashamed of what dad was doing to me that I begged him not to tell my mother? Where was God when I was being raped while my father watched and then took his turn? Where was God when I was tied up and beaten with a riding crop until I was black and blue? Where was God when my body betrayed me, and brought me shame, by responding when I didn't want it to? Where was God when I cried out in despair and wanted to simply give up living?

We need to forgive ourselves. We need to forgive others. And, we need to forgive God. Not for His sake, but for ours. In the words of Mahatma Gandhi, *"The weak can never forgive. Forgiveness is the attribute of the strong."*

Playing the victim role allows us to hold on to anger and blame someone or something else for what happened to us. Norman Vincent Peale said, *"Many people suffer poor health not because of what they eat but from what is eating them. If you are harboring any ill will or resentment or grudges, cast them out. Get rid of them without delay. They do not hurt anybody else. They do no harm to the person against whom you hold these feelings, but every day and every night of your life they are eating at you."*

Sometimes, we suffer consequences from the decisions of someone else. Sometimes, we suffer from the consequences of our own mistakes and decisions. Sometimes, terrible things happen to those who don't deserve it.

I love the story of Job in the Bible. Whenever I start feeling sorry for myself, I remember Job and how he suffered because Satan wanted to test him. Job lost almost everything. He lost his home, his children, and his land. He suffered from boils all over his body. His friends and wife told him to curse God. But, he would not. Job knew God is the source for good not evil. Job questioned God, but then he repented. God restored him in the end.

It's natural to have doubts or to want to question God. As John C. Maxwell says, *"God doesn't mind questions; it's doubt that He hates...No matter how dark our circumstances may grow, we must resist the temptation to doubt God's holy nature."*

We are human. We all make mistakes. Remember, the bigger the battle, the greater the victory when we do overcome.

God doesn't cause the pain in our lives. God didn't cause my dad to do what he did or my mom to stand by him. God gives us the freedom to choose for ourselves. Satan tempts us to make the wrong choices. We live on earth with pain, suffering, and sin. Bad things will happen to good people. I had to learn to let go of my anger and stop blaming God for my situation. I learned we sometimes pray for a miracle, and the answer is no.

Today, I still pray for miracles, but I also pray for peace with God's answer.

Excerpt from *Ria's Story From Ashes To Beauty*, by Ria Story

A LOST SOUL

My life went from bad to worse. Within weeks of the rape, I was given a wedding ring to wear whenever we were in public, but not around family. I felt like a piece of property, and I was emotionally blackmailed into going along with everything. I was convinced I was supposed to think my purpose in life was to make my father happy. Yet deep down, I was struggling because I knew it wasn't right. I would cry myself to sleep many nights and try to be tough during the day. Dad was a master at manipulating my emotions to make me feel sorry for him and then guilty for trying to stop him. He always said the only way he was going to be able to go to Heaven was if I didn't tell anyone what was going on. If I told, that meant he would go to Hell, so it was my responsibility to make sure he wasn't condemned eternally.

He spent endless hours *"talking"* to me, while I studied the wallpaper patterns and tried to shut everything out. I learned to just shut down emotionally and retreat to a secret place inside my heart. My safe place.

READ MORE BOOKS BY RIA

In *Beyond Bound and Broken*, Ria shares how she overcame shame, fear, and doubt stemming from years of being sexually abused by her father. Forced to play the role of a wife and even shared with other men due to her father's perversions, Ria left home at 19 without a job, a car, or even a high-school diploma. This book contains lessons on resilience and overcoming adversity that you can apply in your own life.

In *Ria's Story From Ashes To Beauty*, Ria tells her story of growing up as a victim of sexual abuse from age 12 – 19, and leaving home to escape. She shares how she went on to thrive and learn to help others by sharing her story.

READ MORE BOOKS BY RIA

The Effective Leadership Series books are written to develop and enhance your leadership skills while also helping you increase your abilities in areas like communication and relationships, time management, planning and execution, and leading and implementing change. Look for more books in the Effective Leadership Series:

- *Straight Talk: The Power of Effective Communication*
- *Change Happens: Leading Yourself and Others through Change*
- *PRIME Time: The Power of Effective Planning*
- *Leadership Gems for Women: 30 Characteristics of Very Successful Women*
- *Leadership Gems: 30 Characteristics of Very Successful Leaders*

READ MORE BOOKS BY RIA

Women are naturally high level leaders because they are relationship oriented. However, it's a *"man's world"* out there and natural ability isn't enough to help you be successful as a leader. You must intentionally develop your skills, so you can lead and influence others at home, at work, at church, or even as a volunteer.

In *Leadership Gems For Women*, Ria has packed 30 precious gems of leadership wisdom on characteristics of very successful women - and insight on how you can develop them yourself. Ria has combined her years of experience in leadership roles of different organizations along with years of studying, teaching, training, and speaking on leadership to give you 30 short and simple, yet powerful and profound, lessons to help you become very successful, regardless of whether you are in a formal leadership position or not.

READ MORE BOOKS BY RIA

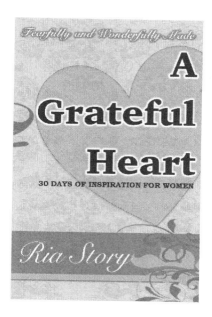

Become inspired by this 30-day collection of daily devotions for women, where you will find practical advice on intentionally living with a grateful heart, inspirational quotes, short journaling opportunities, and scripture from God's Word on practicing gratitude.

READ BOOKS BY MACK STORY

Blue-Collar Leadership and *Blue-Collar Leadership and Supervision* are written specifically for those on the front lines of the Blue-Collar workforce and those who lead them. With 30 short, easy to read chapters, the *Blue-Collar Leadership Series* books contain powerful leadership lessons in a simple and easy to understand format.

Visit www.BlueCollarLeadership.com to learn more, get your free download of the first five chapters from both books, watch Mack's related video series, and listen to podcasts.

READ BOOKS BY MACK STORY

Mack's *MAXIMIZE Your Potential* and *MAXIMIZE Your Leadership Potential* books are the white-collar version of the *Blue-Collar Leadership Series*. These books are written specifically for those working on the front lines and those who lead them. With 30 short, easy to read chapters, they contain powerful leadership lessons in a simple and easy to understand format.

Everything rises and falls on influence. Nothing will impact your professional and personal life more than your ability to influence others. Are you looking for better results in your life, team, or organization? In *Defining Influence*, everyone at all levels will learn the keys to intentionally increasing your influence in all situations from wherever you are.

READ BOOKS BY MACK STORY

It's no longer *"Buyer Beware!"* It's *"Seller Beware!"* Why? Today, the buyer has the advantage over the seller. Most often, they are holding it in their hand. It's a smart phone. They can learn everything about your product before they meet you. The major advantage you do still have is: YOU!

This book is filled with 30 short chapters providing unique insights that will give you the advantage, not over the buyer, but over your competition: those who are selling what you're selling. It will help you sell yourself.

READ BOOKS BY MACK STORY

The *10 Values of High Impact Leaders* will help you lead with speed and develop 360° of influence from wherever you are. High impact leaders align their habits with key values in order to maximize their influence.

10 Foundational Elements of Intentional Transformation is a *"how-to"* roadmap of transformation. The principles Mack shares in this book are the principles he personally applied to transform his life, his career, and his relationships, both personally and professionally.